> **the elements of**

# the aborigine
# tradition

## james g cowan

ELEMENT

Shaftesbury, Dorset • Rockport • Massachusetts • Melbourne, Australia

© Element Books Limited, 1992
Text © James G. Cowan 1992

First published in Great Britain in 1992 by
Element Books Limited
Shaftesbury, Dorset SP7 8BP

Published in the USA in 1992 by
Element Books, Inc.
PO Box 830, Rockport, MA 01966

Published in Australia in 1992 by
Element Books and
distributed by Penguin Books Australia Limited
487 Maroondah Highway, Ringwood,
Victoria 3134

Reprinted March and November 1994

Reissued 1997

Cover design by Max Fairbrother
Typeset by Falcon Typographic Art Ltd, Edinburgh
Printed and bound in Great Britain by
Biddles Ltd, Guildford & Kings Lynn

British Library Cataloguing in Publication
data available

Library of Congress Cataloging in Publication
data available

ISBN 1–86204–144X

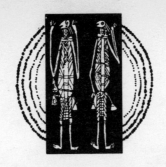

# CONTENTS

For Kathleen Raine, *Vates*

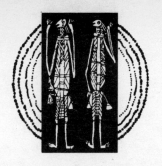

# INTRODUCTION

The Australian Aborigines are a traditional people whose origins lie in distant antiquity. Where they come from and how they came to be in Australia is still a matter of learned conjecture as these people chose not to record their heritage, except in the form of myth and story. Their lives are rich in myth even today which has, of course, contributed to the perception that they are a strange, Stone Age people with undeveloped sensibilites. The idea that they owe allegiance to no political organization, that they worship numerous spirits, and that they practise obscure, secretive rites, has branded them as being prehistoric in the eyes of many. The truth is that Australian Aborigines represent the conscience of us all as they recognize and acknowledge at all times the metaphysical origins of the human spirit.

It is with this in mind that I have attempted to explore certain key aspects of Aboriginal Tradition which I believe form the basis of their way of life. This way of life, or their mode of existence prior to European contact 200 years ago, is now under threat – indeed some might say all but extinct. Many Aborigines have succumbed to the debilitations of modern existence, choosing instead to eke out a degraded form of survival in whichever way they can. This is not their fault, but the fault of pressure brought to bear upon them by the invading white culture eager to take away their birthright – that is, the land itself. It is true to say that until recently Aborigines were not considered to have any right to the land they had inhabited for countless millenia. Instead they were seen as nomads, people who could be moved on – or off – the land that they considered inseparable from their soul.

Of course, the law has changed. Aborigines do have legal status as citizens nowadays. But the original land grab has not yet been fully acknowledged, either by state or federal governments. Certain areas have been set aside as Aboriginal territory, but even these are looked upon with covert eyes by mining company executives and oil-drilling operators. At the time of writing, Kakadu National Park in the Northern Territory, once a pristine environment of immense beauty, is now home to a major uranium mine, complete with radioactive spills into the surrounding creeks during the wet season (all regarded as 'unrepeatable' accidents), and a long-running dispute over the right to mine a sacred place for gold by Pancontinental, at a place known as Coronation Peak. Wherever there is the prospect of a company recording a large economic return then, invariably, the integrity of Aboriginal land is brought into question. Mining company executives are unable to estimate the value of myth, but they can quantify the National Estate in terms of export dollars and stockholder dividends.

Aboriginal spirituality is a haven for the mysterious. In their beliefs we can the find origins of ourselves as a people who are capable of more than just a material existence. During the course of their stay in Australia, they have managed to build up countless natural libraries of their religious history – on cave walls, rock faces and land forms, among ravines and mountains, in the lives of animals and birds, trees and insects, fish and sea mammals, even among the stars overhead. They have studied nature, drawn their conclusions from it, and found it to be the embodiment of a profound metaphysical principal pertaining to all existence. For they have seen in nature much more than its visible beauty, fraternity and practical purpose as a provider. They have seen in it a symbol of an underlying reality which needs to be understood as sacred if true wisdom is to be attained. Their knowledge of nature as symbolic of the divine therefore makes them sages of a kind who, unfortunately, grace this earth less and less.

In the past, too, Aborigines have found themselves the victims of social, scientific and anthropological studies which tended to overemphasize, and indeed highlight, their differences from the rest of humanity, particularly modern humanity. Ritual practices which appeared to confirm their Stone Age mentality, or the complexity of their familial relationships, were made icons of cultural backwardness in order to affirm, at least implicitly, modern perceptions of cultural superiority. These, in turn, became the basis for justifying Aboriginal cultural assimilation into the white man's world, their early disenfranchisement, and their subsequent oppression as a minority race. The world found itself left with an ancient culture permanently disfigured by genocide and racism as a result.

In truth, the Aboriginal people of Australia offer us a parable for survival. In spite of everything, they cling to their cultural heritage against all attempts to demean it by way of well-meaning endeavour, government interference, inoperative health programmes and the ever present spectre of mining companies wishing to encroach upon their land. They are a courageous people who have managed to survive *because* of, not in spite of their luminous spiritual heritage. For it is the knowledge that the Rainbow Snake and the Lightning Brothers, the Mimi People and the Maletji Law Dogs, the Wanbanbiries and Marlu, the Great Kangaroo, the Ninja Ice Men and the Pungalunga Men, the Waugeluk Sisters and Mingala, the First Man are still alive – all these and so many more spirit entities throughout the land – which makes it possible for the Aborigines to remain optimistic about their future. Because it is such mythic personages who sustain them during these dark hours when the truth of spiritual knowledge is questioned so readily by present-day humanists and scientists alike.

This book, therefore, represents a small attempt to protect one of the world's oldest spiritual heritages. It is my belief that without such heritages the world will soon wither and die at its root. One of my Aboriginal informants expressed it more poignantly when he said, 'We don't sing the songs anymore. And when we don't sing the songs, the animals soon leave. That what we doin' to the world: lettin' nature go off to die. Because we don't sing the songs.' In an age when all the tunes are called by the scientists, economists, and government planners bent on budget balancing and the development of new technology, we find ourselves listening to the shrill sound of progress at the expense of that Aboriginal threnody, expressive of myth and wonder, which is now lamenting the spiritual demise of their people. The Aborigines, with their inexhaustible capacity for forbearance, are still pleading with us to listen to what they have to say, even as we refuse to to do so.

What they have to say is relatively simple: that they have as much right to live in this world *on their own terms* as modern humankind has. In other words – and they speak for all traditional peoples – no one group of people has the right to foist upon another a cultural viewpoint foreign to their own. This is at the very heart of the modern dilemma. Wherever material values and the philosophy of growth dominate, we find a desire to overrule all those who speak from the perspective of non-materialism and non-growth. In Australia this argument is fought out between mining company executives, government servants and pastoralists in one corner, and a culturally isolated race of people in the other. No wonder the Aborigines find themselves branded as backward, irresponsible, with no respect for the 'national interest'. They are seen as the last bastion of prehistory which stands between modern man and his desire to exploit the land. Unfortunately, all the forces of modern society are arraigned against them, and they are unlikely to withstand the bombardment.

Aboriginal tradition represents one of our last links with a genuinely theocentric way of life. When we destroy this, we destroy the knowledge inherent to this lifestyle. We also destroy the validity of myth and the interdependence of man and nature which myth illuminates. For myth invokes a spiritual bond between ourselves and the earth. It is this bond that Aborigines have always observed, feeling themselves heirs to a celestial landscape which must be handed on in the same pristine condition as it came down to them. They recognize also how important it is to acknowledge the 'priority of the past' and its claim to the truths imbued in landscape. The Ancestors, the Old Ones, who have gone before – these people still exist as metaphysical entities in the landscape itself. Thus to destroy the earth – that is, to dig it up or deface it for material

4

ends – is to eliminate forever their invisible reality as prophets (*kahins*) for those who are alive today. When the Ancestors are reduced to gold ingots, uranium yellowcake or iron ore, then the process of destruction has advanced beyond recall. In this respect the local Aborigines, to whom Coronation Peak is a sacred place, prophesy the 'destruction of the world' by malign forces if the site should be tampered with in any way.

What the Aborigines stand for is the need for traditional wisdoms to retain a validity and remain intrinsic to our philosophic and scientific perceptions of the cosmos. We cannot do without their knowledge, their spiritual perspective, their deep faith in the harmony of all nature. If we ignore these qualities, we do so at the risk of making nature our enemy. Perhaps it will not rise up against us today; but tomorrow the likelihood of our survival will be severely tested. The destruction of the ozone layer, global warming, environmental pollution, the exhaustion of nature's resources, overpopulation and the appearance of virulent new diseases among us – these are but a few of the symptoms of the Earth's experiences as we continue to mistreat it in order to satisfy our own ends. The Aborigines are pleading with us to cease our actions before it is too late. Excavating Coronation Peak, the 'crown' of God's Creation so to speak, has become the metaphor for our own self-destruction.

Over the years I have worked with a number of Aboriginal communities throughout Australia. From the far north to the far west I have travelled among them – around Arnhemland, the Kimberley, the Pilbara, about the Centre, in the McDonnell Ranges and west of Haast Bluff, among the crags of Carnarvon Gorge, Mootwingee and Uluru, on islands such as Depuch and in the Torres Strait. All these places have become a part of my spiritual homeland. I have spoken with old men who still remember the days when the Law meant something. People like Banjo Woonamurra, Roger and James Solomon, David Mowaljarlai, Bill Idumdum, Toby Kangale, Bill Neidjie, Woodley King, Larry Woonamurra, Nebo and Binny have all contributed to my knowledge of their culture. In the process I have become, in a sense, 'Aboriginalized', absorbing into myself a way of looking upon the world which is uniquely theirs. Now the Rainbow Snake and the Lightning Brothers are part of my own spiritual pantheon. I no longer feel that exclusivity of belief is necessary in order to live a genuinely religious life. Indeed, if an Aborigine can absorb the teachings of the Gospels into his life, why can't I absorb those of Marlu, the Great Kangaroo, or the Maletji Law Dogs into mine?

I hope this book will encourage the reader to pursue his or her studies further in the field of traditional wisdom. It is a field that offers the prospect of a bountiful harvest. All landscapes are celestial, and all people who revere their environment can consider themselves half man, half god as did Gilgamesh, the Sumerian hero of old. It is up to each reader to encounter his own wild man, his own Enkidu, within himself, and wrestle him to a standstill. Then, perhaps, the future of traditional wisdom and traditional cultures such as the Aborigines' will flourish in the world once more.

*James G. Cowan*

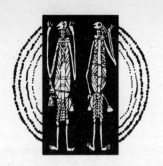

# 1 · BRIDGING THE GAP

On a spring morning in 1968 Dr Jim Bowler, a geomorphologist, made a remarkable find. While studying sediments in the Willandra Lakes region of central New South Wales, Australia, he discovered what appeared to be stone artefacts and mussel shells, suggesting a human presence on the dry bed of Lake Mungo. He also noticed some burnt, carbon-encrusted bones protruding from a low hummock on the dunes. These were later excavated and carbon dated back in Canberra. They were confirmed to be over 26,000 years old.

Suddenly Australia seemed far older in terms of human habitation than any other place on earth. Subsequent excavations in 1974 brought to light the oldest complete human skeleton yet found. Known as Mungo Man III, his delicate, gracile figure had lain buried in the sands of the lake for 30,000 years, hands clasped in front in a perfect state of repose. Traces of red ochre were found encrusted on his bones. It was clear that our Pleistocene forebear had been buried with the full benefit of mortuary rites, intimating that Mungo Man III was heir to a significant spiritual tradition previously considered to be a more recent acquisition. The mummies of ancient Egypt now found their prototype in the dunes of Lake Mungo.[1] Furthermore, it became evident that

Aboriginal Australians held in trust, unbroken and pristine so to speak, the oldest living culture.

## ORIGINS OF ABORIGINAL CULTURE

The legacy of this ancient way of life is still with us. Coming to terms with such antiquity is not always easy, given our reliance upon oral records and the testimony of numerous steles and temple walls in Egypt and Sumeria. The Aborigines speak to us with a knowledge that reaches back to Mungo Man and beyond. Complex mortuary rites are implied on every ochred bone. A timeless culture is suggested in the way he lies so gracefully in the earth. No man addresses us with such eloquence on the subject of the origins of spirituality and custom as he does. Instead of asking ourselves, where did the Egyptians gain their architectural knowledge? we must first ask ourselves: where did the Aborigine come from, how did he acquire his metaphysical gift, and what part did Australia play in forming his spiritual world? Answering such questions as these might help us develop a deeper understanding of our human origins in other parts of the world.

A number of models have been put forward as to the peopling of Australia. These are largely conditioned by geological evidence, confirming that fifty million years ago Australia was a part of Antarctica. A continental breakaway and subsequent drift northward was further complicated by post-Ice Age inundation which isolated the land mass as late as 120,000 years ago. Although the sea has fallen and risen and fallen again as recently as 20,000 years ago, Australia's essential isolation from the rest of the evolving land masses of the world has remained. Even when the sea level was at its lowest there was never a complete land bridge linking Australia to Southeast Asia. The result is that the country has continued to exist as an ancient micro-environment where a variety of species which had become extinct elsewhere were able to survive to this day.

It is important to understand how distinct Australia is from the rest of the world if we are to comprehend the unique contribution that Aborigines have made to the genesis of early thought and spirituality. This is not to say that Aborigines were or are different to other people, but only to recognize the influences which have helped to form their personal vision. We know, for example, that modern man first appeared in the world little more than 250,000 years ago. Research now tells us that the first people landed in Australia some 200,000 years later, which means these early migrants arrived with a considerable body of knowledge, customs, and ritual practices from which to draw strength and confidence. They did not arrive in Australia devoid of any civilizing influence. Nor did they arrive by accident.

At a time when the sea was at its lowest level (some 50 metres lower than it is today) Australia and New Guinea were linked by the Sahul Shelf, a low plain which would have brought the southern islands of Indonesia to within less than 100 kilometres from the Kimberley coastline. Island hopping from Southeast Asia would have involved no more than eight sea voyages of between 30 and 87 kilometres. Reaching Timor, it would have been possible for the nomads to recognize the smoke from distant bushfires on continental Australia, caused by lightning as it ignited dry vegetation.[2] Such smoke plumes are visible up to 110 kilometres away. Even the glare of these bushfires could have been visible at night on Timor and other nearby islands.

Curiosity or inclement weather might have prompted a southern sea voyage towards Australia. We have no record of prehistoric boats, so we must assume that the first arrivals reached Australia on rafts made from bamboo or mangrove wood. Tidal movement in the tropics is considerable, and a drifting raft could easily have been drawn into the orbit of mainland Australia. As castaways or as genuine migrants, the first people would have found it difficult to return across the Arafura Sea to their homeland. In any event we do not know whether they wanted to. As hunter-gatherers, they would have probably looked upon Australia as a rich source of food. Without competition from neighbouring tribes and with the presence of plentiful game and few carnivores to threaten them, the first people would have quickly accepted their new home and, in time, adapted to the unique opportunities it presented.

Culturally or ethnically we do not know where Aborigines

came from. Genetic evidence does not link them either to the Veddoid peoples of India or Sri Lanka, nor to the Ainu of northern Japan. However, recent molecular biological studies suggest that the Australian-Oriental lineage diverged about 40,000 years ago. All of which means that it is likely that Aborigines came from somewhere in Asia, and carried with them to their new homeland vestiges of prehistoric Oriental culture. What they did with this knowledge over subsequent millenia resulted in the Aborigines' world picture.

This is not to say that Mungo Man's antecedents were the *only* migrants. At a place known as Kow Swamp in Victoria some bones, including the skull of a massive, archaic-featured man, were uncovered in what later turned out to be a grave site for twelve other people. Though carbon dated at between 9000 and 15,000 years old, the bones indicated the existence of a different, perhaps earlier genus of man living alongside Mungo Man. It seems that two types of people had shared the land in those days, not only in isolated pockets in the north as assumed, but all over the country. Again, the Kow Swamp people had shown signs of being formally buried, indicating the observance of ritual and therefore a vision of meaning to life and death. Traces of resin on kangaroo teeth confirmed regalia had been buried alongside their owners. But a question remained: did the Kow Swamp people finally merge with the Mungo Man people and disappear?[3] All we do know for certain is that the first people, whoever they were, had already wandered far afield in search of sustenance. Australia was populated not only by different peoples who might have arrived in subsequent millenia, but by the different intellectual concepts, beliefs and customs they had brought with them.

It is at this point that we begin to see the confrontation of a people of Asian origin with a landscape totally different to one they had previously experienced. Australia's isolation had produced a living environment unlike any other place left on earth. The age of the dinosaurs had long since passed, leaving only their frozen footprints and a few petrified bones to indicate their earlier presence. But what did remain, as testimony to the slow processes of evolution, were a genus of non-placental animals, known as marsupials. The first people, too, would have encountered the last species of mega-fauna to survive on earth, animals such as giant kangaroo (procoptodon), and the largest of all, the wombat or diprotodon – an animal the size of a rhinoceros. Most of these animals, however, were herbivorous, thus posing little or no threat to Aborigines. Only the crocodile and a large marsupial hunter, the thylacoleo, was any real threat. Seven-foot-long lizards, known as goannas, might have also proved difficult to overcome with spear or stone axe.

But as these died out, due to climatic changes and the increasing aridity of the inland, the Aborigines found themselves masters of a remote continent filled with ancient geological outcrops, like Ayers Rock (Uluru) and the Olgas (Katatjuta). With slow-changing river systems, huge lakes which periodically dried up, and low mountain ranges all but immune from volcanic activity, the Aborigines found themselves inhabiting a country whose hallmark was geological stability. For the most part the country generated a timeless certainty born from a sense of resolution. Australia, unlike many other continents afflicted by earth tremors and intense volcanic activity, had simply grown old. Rounded hills, well-weathered ridges, endless plains and an uncluttered coastline gave the country something of a worn appearance. It represented for those early inhabitants stability, perpetuity and silence. Rapid change was not a factor in the formation of the continent – at least, not in the eyes of its first inhabitants. Such stability, therefore, became as much a part of the Aboriginal character as any earlier traits they might have brought with them from the north. It made them conservative and inward looking, a race content to generate their own spiritual reality out of the lonely nature of the land they had chosen to settle.

It is important to understand the environmental conditions under which Aborigines began their occupation of the continent. Some thousands of years were to pass before the entire country was to experience human habitation. Travelling out from the Kimberley coast and Cape York Peninsula, the Pleistocene nomads would have followed river systems from their estuaries deep inland. As they became accustomed to surviving in an often harsh environment, so too would they have foraged further afield. In the process they would have had to enter into a metaphysical dialogue with a hitherto unknown land. This was inevitable given how forbidding the wilderness would have appeared to the intruder. Even today, walking through such places without knowledge of their sacred lore may often provoke a feeling of strangeness, even hostility. It is a condition that the early inhabitants must have frequently experienced as they claimed each new territory as their own.

How they overcame this feeling of alienation is essential to the understanding of the Aborigine's unique relationship with his land. This will be discussed in greater detail in Chapter 5, but it is true to say that they 'mapped' their territory with the same vigour as any modern-day cartographer. Not a tree, cave, rockhole, saltpan, creek bed or outcrop escaped their notice when it came to recording the features of their tribal land. In fact, so complete was their knowledge of their country that it could be reduced to a series of symbols or zigzag markings, either on a sand drawing or a war shield.

One investigator[4] discovered far more than he bargained for when he interviewed an elderly Ngarluma *mekigar* or medicine man of the Pilbara (Western Australia) in 1967 on the subject of these war shields. Assuming the markings to be merely decorative, he was soon informed by Parraruru that the zigzag flutings, known as *thurrgul* or 'straights', and the *wangu* or 'bends' (ochred red and white) represented a diagrammatic sectional rendition of the Fortesque River from its source to its outflow (see Fig. 1). By looking at the war shield of any warrior living along the river another warrior would know exactly from which bend or waterhole the former came. He could then 'recognize' the man, even if he did not already know him. The shield became the symbolic definition of a totemic environment that not only placed a man *in situ* but also reflected the world-creation process of the Rainbow Snake (see Chapter 2) as it made its way inland from the ocean. In the words of a Jindjiparndi song,[5]

> The snake got up, got up from the north and made a deep trench in the land, digging it halfways, and came along the river from the north. He cut off two halves (of its halfway course) by making waterholes beginning at the edge.

Thus a link was automatically made between the physical aspect of the river in question and its mythological creation.

Furthermore, it was discovered that Aborigines possess absolute 'compass sense' when it came to moving about. That is, they are able to traverse great distances without getting lost. Of course they are familiar with natural features and so identify where they might be by these. But it was also confirmed that when shipped to hospital many hundreds of miles away from their home, Aboriginal patients could point to where 'home' was through the wall of their room. Even blind men rarely err in pointing out a compass bearing. They also refer to compass points in their own language. For example, one doesn't just fall or lie down; one falls north or lies down south, depending on the direction.[6]

Clearly the early inhabitants of Australia had learnt complex techniques of navigation and mapping which were handed down to subsequent generations. These travelling aids were an important way of coming to terms with the remoteness

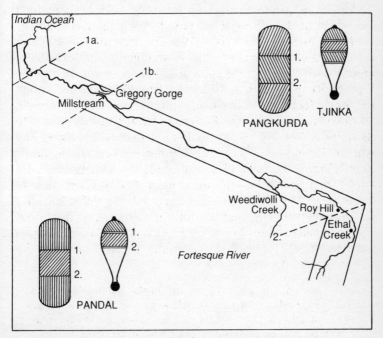

Fig. 1   Shield markings in relation to river bends. (After C. G. von Brandenstein, in *Narratives from the North West of Western Australia in the Ngarluma and Jindjiparndi Languages.*)

of Australia. Shields or sand drawings (also message sticks and clubs) formed a geographic map of regions from which trading parties or visitors could draw knowledge when it came to travelling through unfamiliar territory. The pristine world of plain, mountain range or river could be represented abstractly and symbolically according to the part it played in the mythological cycle known as the *Alcheringa* or Dreaming.[7]

## THE MYTH CYCLE OF THE DREAMING

The Aborigines did not, however, fail to record the significant climatic changes or the extinction of the last of the mega-fauna. In their myths mention is often made of a time (the Dreaming) before men had peopled the continent when the Sky Heroes were forced to confront such changes. Among the Unda Gnoora tribe of the Cooper region in Central Australia they talk of a time when the dry lake systems were once well watered and fertile. Dense cloud habitually shielded the earth from the sun. Giant gum trees growing nearby drew their sustenance from cooling rains. The unending stony desert of today was then an immense garden.

About that time the Kadimakara, a band of celestial heroes, came down from their leafy home in the trees. They were drawn to the verdant pasture below. The three gum trees down which they had climbed (pillars holding up the sky) were then mysteriously destroyed. Cut off from their celestial home the Kadimakara were forced to roam about the lower world, wallowing in the marshes until they eventually died. Their remains were petrified in the salt lake of Callabonna until they were 'discovered' by a museum team in 1893. Scientifically named 'diprotodon' (giant wombat), one of the skeletons of a Kadimakara now graces an exhibit in Adelaide.

But the story does not end here. The small holes in the sky left by the gum trees' absence gradually increased in size until they merged to form one big hole known as 'Puri Wilpanina' or the 'Great Hole'. In the intervening millennia since the appearance of the Great Hole, the country was wracked by a succession of droughts and floods. Meanwhile, the Unda Gnoora, the first human inhabitants who now existed on Earth, found themselves threatened by one catastrophe after another.

Either their hunting grounds were under water due to flood, or the wildlife they depended upon for food had departed in the wake of yet another drought.[8]

Such a myth reflects the significant climatic changes that occured millions of years ago when Lake Walloon was formed in the interior. Before that, lush forests, populated by diprotodons, flamingoes, and later, in the lake itself, dolphins and lungfish flourished. When Lake Walloon dried up, leaving only a few salt lakes behind, Australia entered a new phase – one that the Aborigines of the interior confronted in the form of an increasingly arid environment which demanded of them all their ingenuity to survive. The myth of the Kadimakara tells of a time when abundance reigned, only to be destroyed by the excessive demands made upon the environment by the Sky Heroes' insatiable appetites. It is a lesson all Aborigines have learned.

In contrast, the rising of the waters, presumably at the end of an Ice Age, is recorded in a Northern Territory myth related by a member of the Murinbata tribe. He tells of how continuous rain resulted in the land becoming submerged under a rising sea. Only one mountain top remained above the waterline to which all the men of the bird totems, under the command of the stone-curlew man, Karen, were guided. Together they built a dam of stones about their island to keep out the rising waters. Those animals that managed to swim to the safety of the island provided the castaways with food. It is said that these animals were men who had changed into their totemic form. Eventually Karen ordered bird-men to fly out and reconnoitre the ocean to see whether any land was showing. When they returned without news of land, Karen sent out two honey-eater bird-men in the hope that they might bring back better news. After a day and night at sea, the honey-eater bird-men finally returned with a branch of leaves in their beaks. To celebrate their discovery, and the knowledge that survival was assured, Karen flew high into the sky, where he became a star close to the moon. After the waters had receded the bird-men became birds and flew back to their tribal countries.[9]

The story is similar to that of Noah and the Ark: how birds and animals of different species clustered together on a tiny island like Noah in his ark in order to escape the flood.

Presumably Ice Age inundation caused similar disruptions to the lives of men and animals at various times. What this Northern Territory myth does is describe such a cataclysm, and how all life struggled to survive.

## SPIRIT OF PLACE

From the very beginning the first people embarked upon a process of integration with their new land. Learning to recognize climate changes, understanding the habits of unusual fauna, coming to terms with the nutritional and medicinal properties of a wild and antique flora – these were some of the tasks that confronted the first people as they moved southward across the continent. Like later European explorers who rode into the outback on horse and camel, they also 'named' places in an act of self-identification. The difference, however, lay in the way the earlier migrants encased the land in a mythological envelope, thus securing it in what became a timeless reality which would serve as spiritual sustenance to the countless generations that followed.

Here we must digress. To understand the process of making the land the focus of metaphysical or mystical insight is the key to understanding Aboriginal religious belief. As they were initially a migrant culture, the Aborigines brought with them many concepts formed elsewhere. These had to be grafted on to their new environment in a way that made existence fulfilling in its deepest sense. To argue that they were likely to be awed by natural phenomena because they could not explain them is, in the words of Ludwig Wittgenstein, a 'stupid superstition of our time'. Furthermore, it is evident that religious responses derive from the possibilities in the language and life of a people.[10] How the Aborigines addressed their new land, if not in words and mystical concepts, then in its *symbolic* form, is important in understanding what Henry Corbin called 'visionary geography'.[11]

Among Aborigines the earth embodies a culture of its own. It was formed, after all, by the explicit action of Sky Heroes at the time of the Dreaming. Thus the land is a geographical icon because its very coming into being is of a mystical order, not a geological one. Its categories of sacredness, recognizable as they are by the intellect or soul, can be seen in the landscape. This means that the earth becomes not only representative of the ideal but the manifest form. In the Aboriginal context this is a 'Dreaming landscape', an embodiment of mystical realities not easily explained by language. So that when an Aborigine speaks of his 'Dreaming' he is talking about the land as an icon which expresses his mystical attachment to it. His whole being, his cultural associations and knowledge of tribal law, which have been handed down to him from the Dreaming, become an extension of the visionary geography to which he ascribes.

The Aborigine's deep reverence for his tribal country is the result of the first people's encounter with its very *newness* as a metaphysical concept, rather than its great age in the geological sense. Bridging the gap between the Pleistocene culture of some anonymous Asian country and the lonely, unpeopled landscape of Australia demanded a special kind of commitment from the original migrants. Formulating a canon of belief capable of sustaining them in their new environment is only one aspect of the intellectual leap that must have occured during the first 10,000 years of colonization and settlement. Developing a body of myths, songs and dances as well as the various answers required to explain the origin of useful implements such as spear, axe or boomerang demanded considerable thought if they were to retain their 'magical' properties as cultural artefacts. For it is clear that the Aborigine did not distinguish between the metaphysical dimension as the source of all knowledge and the physical domain. To him they were one and the same: nature's manifestation was as a result of the metaphysical stimulus, not as a result of the operation of physical forces.

Nevertheless, as a nomadic band of hunter-gatherers, the Aborigines embarked upon the task of naming and categorizing things in accordance with their spiritual and nutritional requirements. Nature's realm yielded up new configurations of flora and fauna which needed to be addressed. At the same time they were called upon to 'explain' their own origins in terms of their earlier migrant status, as well as in terms of their status as beings of a spiritual order. These dual explanations often went hand in hand so long as one resorted to tribal myth to provide answers. It is clear from the myths of many northern tribes that they were conscious of the first people, their forebears, coming from across the water. The story of the Maletji dogs of the Kimberley region of northwest Australia indicates the arrival of the dingo (a wild dog distantly related to the pariah dog of India) said to have reached Australian shores approximately 4000 years ago. Conversely, it may well embody for Aborigines a deeply felt, though rarely stated, belief in their early migrant status.

In any event, the Maletji dogs were said to have swum the Indian Ocean in order to reach an offshore island in the King Sound area. From here they had waded ashore on the mainland and travelled southwest between Napier and the King Leopold Ranges, creating the landscape wherever they scratched for water. Reaching the present-day Fitzroy Crossing, close to the northern perimeter of the Great Sandy Desert, they encountered a westerly wind which carried the scent of water. This they followed back along the Napier Range, passing through Windjana Gorge along the northern face to the scent source, the Perilama rockhole at Barralumma. Here they decided to stay where there was a ready food supply in the form of animals coming in to drink. They exist today as self-painted 'shadows' on the rock face.

Such a story is a mine of interesting information pertaining to the literal movement of dingoes in their search for water once they had arrived in Australia. It also accounts for the creation of waterholes or, more particularly, the logic of animal trails between waterholes – trails that Aborigines use also as they traverse their country. Significantly, the Maletji dogs are found all over the inland desert region. An increase site celebrating their continued renewal can be found at Ngama cave in the Tanami Desert, more than 1000 kilometres southeast of the Kimberley. These dogs also accompanied Jarapiri, the Great Snake (otherwise known as the Rainbow Snake or by regional names such as Warlu and Kunukban, amongst others) from Winbaraku further south to Ngama at the time of the Dreaming.[12] The many myths and stories associated with the Maletji dogs places them in a special category of Sky Heroes who are responsible for world creation as a primal event.

But there exists another dimension to the Dream Journey of

the Maletji dogs. According to an elderly Bunuba tribesman, Banjo Woonamurra, these dogs were also responsible, at least in part, for the dissemination of Aboriginal law.[13] Whether they brought this law with them from a far shore, or whether those early migrants responsible for the dingo's arrival in Australia are the principal law custodians is unclear. And so it should be. The process of mythologization has subsumed the separate ingredients that make up the story of the Maletji dogs and transformed them into fact. The Maletji dogs have transcended their dingo and migrant status and become instead bearers of godlike spirit. For this reason the dingo holds a special place in the hearts of Aborigines, both as a pet, hunting aid, a blanket on winter nights and the embodiment of tribal law. Its increase or *thallu* sites are found all over the country.

Australia's isolation from the rest of the world made unusual demands upon its early inhabitants. Lacking any cross-fertilization from large tribal migrations, the Aborigines soon settled into a way of life whose principal characteristic was a rejection of innovation and change. The continuing presence of a Stone Age culture in a world that had long

Fig. 2   Maletji Law Dogs, Napier Range, Western Australia.

19

ago committed itself to increasing socialization and material development reflects cultural isolation, of course. But it also reflects the essential rigour of a primordial existence when it is not interfered with from outside. The Aboriginal way of life is both simple and complex, backward in a material sense yet highly evolved in a spiritual sense. These dichotomies sit easily on the shoulders of the Aborigine just so long as he is not forced to subject his culture and belief to the demands made upon it by outsiders. Like many traditional peoples of the world he wishes to live according to priorities which set religious activity above that of material innovation. His 'backwardness', therefore, is in part a choice he has made. Spiritual introversion has given him a strength that precludes any real sympathy for those who suffer discontent at the hands of a more material lifestyle. The land is his saviour and the source of his well-being.

Australia and its original inhabitants offer us a rare opportunity to come to terms with where we have come from. To see this solely in terms of cultural evolution is to miss the point. Stone Age culture is indeed a wild culture. But it also holds certain values which make the act of living supremely worthwhile. Discovering the essential nature of a culture which has chosen to take a separate path from that of our own means that we must first be prepared to bridge the gap separating us from the Palaeolithic vision. The Aborigines do not think differently from us; they merely observe material data in a more mystical way. For them their environment is not and has never come into being as a result of morphic activity. Spiritual identities govern the creation of their world. It is these spiritual identities, or Sky Heroes, which form the basis of all religious belief.

Before one enters this world certain conditions must be embraced. The ability to see contact between the physical and spiritual worlds demands a special kind of perception. I have called this perception the Palaeolithic vision because it seems that Aborigines are privy to a way of looking at the world which draws together all the forces governing the visible and invisible realms. Becoming familiar with the spirit pantheon which augments this realm is important to understanding Aboriginal knowledge. Whether it is in the form of the All-father Ungud, or the Rainbow Snake, Jarapiri, these spiritual identities have a part to play in the creation of the world. More importantly perhaps, they are celestial participants in that ancestral moment known as the Alcheringa or Dreaming.

However long ago it was when the first people arrived on Australian shores is less significant than what has occured since. Devising a spiritual landscape out of the rudimentary material that was there reflects the genius of the Aboriginal people. It is this 'visionary geography' that we will investigate further during the course of the next chapter.

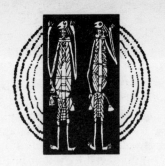

# 2 · In the Footsteps of the Rainbow Snake

It is significant that only in Australia, so far as I am aware, is the rainbow linked to the concept of the Divine Snake. Traditionally a celestial bridge over which only gods might walk (men must walk beneath it), the rainbow has always been regarded as a link between the unseen realm of the Spirit and that of manifestation. The Snake is also considered to be an intermediary between the unmanifest Principle and the realm of matter. According to an early Gnostic text (*Enenchos V, 17,8*)[1] this relationship is confirmed: 'Midway between the Father and Matter . . . the Serpent that moves eternally towards the unmoved Father and moved Matter; now it turns to the Father and gathers up forces in its countenance.' Confronting the Rainbow Snake in the context of Aboriginal cosmology, therefore, represents the merging of two important principles of unity between Spirit and matter. Indeed among the Kogai tribe of Southeast Australia the rainbow was known as *nabal ane tumbila* or 'God his fire.'[2]

More than any other spiritual entity the Rainbow Snake is perhaps the most universal of all among Aborigines. The northern tribes worship its image on cave walls just as the southern tribes do in ritual and rock carving. From the Pilbara in Western Australia to Carnarvon Gorge in Queensland his image can be seen. Around Haast Bluff in Central Australia Jarapiri is said to have emerged from Winbaraku, only to drift northward to a cave at Jukuita in the Tanami Desert. In Mutitjilda Gorge at the foot of Uluru, Wanambi, the Rainbow Snake, sleeps. So does he in Jim Jim Falls on the Arnhemland Escarpment to the north, and at Mootwingee in central New South Wales. Songs celebrate his world-creating effort as do sand paintings fashioned at the time of important tribal ceremonies. No Aborigine will deny the eternal existence of the Great Snake even when they are confronted by the spectre of motor vehicles, social security benefits and the demands made upon them by Christian ethics. Jarapiri transcends all these, a supreme spiritual entity second only to the All-father Ungud (Baiame in eastern Australia, Mangela around the Pilbara, Pundjel in Victoria) himself.

To better understand the Rainbow Snake's significance it is necessary to see how this Spirit entity fits into the metaphysical framework known as the Dreaming. According to one commentator[3] the Alcheringa is 'a cosmogony, an account of the begetting of the universe, a study about creation'. While this might go some way towards explaining the Dreaming, it does not account for its extraordinary importance in the spiritual and social life of the Aborigine. To an earlier observer[4] who had studied the Arunta tribes of Central Australia the Alcheringa was 'the name given to far past times in which the mythical ancestors of the tribe are supposed to have lived'. Among the Nungar of Southwest Australia it was known as *Njidding* (cold or 'ice age'), a period when the 'earth was soft'.[5] Clearly the Dreaming embodies both a historical perspective and an account of First Causes. For it is the activities of the ancestral beings in their various acts of world creation 'outside time' *(illud tempus)* that the Aborigine identifies with when it comes to determining how he should live.

## THE SKY HEROES OF THE DREAMING

Ancestral beings or Sky Heroes take on numerous changeable forms. Their activity around Uluru (Ayers Rock), for example,

23

is explored in a number of major myth cycles relating to the battle between the Liru or poisonous-snake people and the Kunia or carpet-snake people. Mala, the Hare-wallaby people were also decimated by a devil-dog, Kulpunya, before or during the Dreaming in the same region. Further north around Katherine the Lightning Brothers do battle with one another prior to each wet season, while to the west in the Kimberley the mysterious, cloud-like figures known as the Wandjina dominate the beliefs of local tribesmen. Throughout Australia different totemized Sky Heroes take on the form of animals, birds, fish, sea mammals, rocks and sometimes men. Katatjuta (the Olgas) are the metamorphosed bodies of the Pungalunga Men, and at Atila (Mt Conner) the Ninja Ice-men feature in their respective myth cycles.

Since Aborigines are a totemic people it is not surprising that they should regard their Sky Heroes as totemic beings. Or, more precisely, totemic identification has been handed down to Aborigines by the Sky Heroes themselves. It is they who have given form to the living patterns which govern Aboriginal society. The archetypal ideas which form the basis of all living creatures are an essential part of the Sky Heroes' persona, given that they generate 'echoes' of types in the realm of matter. The dictum 'as above, so below' is fully in concordance with the Aboriginal belief in metaphysical exemplars masquerading as Sky Heroes. Thus the Hare-wallaby People or the Pungalunga Men embody both the physical dimension of their earthly prototypes, while at the same time they embody a purely metaphysical dimension that is not and can never be made manifest. The Ninja Ice-men, for example, exist as an Idea representing certain principial values more fully than they do as hoar-frosted beings who sport tinkling icicles in their eyebrows and beards. This image is satisfactory at the exterior level, of course, but it only goes half way to expressing their true reality at the spiritual level.

The Dreaming is, first and foremost, a metaphysical condition denoting the working of divine principles dressed up in the garb of totemic heroes. The myth is their expressive vehicle. Men identify with their Sky Heroes by way of ritual. The great ceremonies central to each tribe act as a channel by which Dreaming events are recalled, contemplated and acted upon in the life of the people. No Aborigine can dismiss the Dreaming without incurring profound psychic disruption. (It is this disruption that is at the root of the urban Aborigine's despair and alienation today. The Dreaming is, unfortunately no longer a living reality for them.) His every action is enveloped in the Dreaming's nurturing capacities from the time of his conception. In this respect Aborigines do not recognize sexual activity as the initiator of conception (except among some northern tribes). Instead they acknowledge that human spirits inhabit the air, waiting to be 'dreamt' into the mother's womb, usually by the woman herself at the behest of a totem or in conjunction with a Dreaming site.[6]

Mountford[7] relates how at Winbaraku, in Ngalia tribal territory in Central Australia, the

> *taraulba* spirit-children live in the storehouse of the sacred objects, the *kulpidjis* [or *Churinga* boards: see Chapter 3] on the summit of Winbaraku. These spirit-children . . . have dark hair with light-coloured streaks in it. The gum on the trunks of the acacia trees provides them with food to eat, and the morning dew with water to drink. Early in the morning the *taraulbas* leave their camp on the summit of Winbaraku and seat themselves in the shade of trees to watch for suitable mothers. When one of them sees a woman to his liking, it reduces itself to the size of a termite, awaiting its opportunity to enter her body. If the little *taraulbas* are unsuccessful on one day, they return to their home on the summit of Winbaraku and resume their quest on the next morning.

Paternity, therefore, is the responsibility of the 'quickening spirit' rather than any physical act on the part of the father. The new life which has chosen to enter the woman is a complete entity who has originated at some time in the long distant past, and is immeasurably more ancient and completely independent of any living person. Nor is the child related by blood to any living person, thus leaving the infant free to form relationships within the tribe that are both spiritual and social.[8]

The presence of the Dreaming in the life of an Aborigine begins, in a sense, before conception. His individual spirit is a part of the infinite reservoir of Spirit that emanates from the Dreaming. His appearance on earth is as a result of a transmigratory act of becoming (manifestation) on the part of spirit entities from the Dreaming. By way of totemic encounter a man is thus 'conceived' in his human form for the duration of his physical life on earth. This means he cannot break the Gordian knot that binds him to the Dreaming. All his life he owes allegiance to the 'spirit that made him' and therefore acknowledges the Dreaming as ever present in his life. In this respect, he may say that such-and-such a person (or place, or indeed himself) is 'in ungud' – that is, in a state of repose, or sanctification, bestowed by the Dreaming itself.

The Dreaming, however, cannot be regarded as a paradisiac state or the reflection of a Golden Age. The Age of Heroes may indeed promote a nostalgia for the past among Aborigines, but such a feeling is governed by the knowledge that the Dreaming events occured in a remote past. Nevertheless, by its very timeless quality, the Dreaming conjures up an immediate present whereby the acts of Sky Heroes are *still* occuring, particularly during ceremonial activity. Aborigines often explain Dreaming events in the present tense, as if they were happening as they spoke. Since neither time nor history exist in any meaningful sense to the Aborigine, it is fitting that the Dreaming should partake of eternality rather than temporality. Nevertheless social time does exist and therefore imposes its round of ceremonies upon the tribal unit. Cyclic time is inherent in the Dreaming, bringing distant events into the immediate present with consumate ease.

This does not mean that the Dreaming cannot be expressed. Long myth cycles detailing the creation of the land by Sky Heroes, ceremonial dances (corroborees) which entail men changing their personas into those of respective Dreaming heroes (painting the body with the designs of the totemic identity ensures that a man has transcended himself), drawing paintings in the sand as adjuncts to ritual – these are but some of the methods by which the Dreaming is given recognizable dimension. Individual artists have also drawn upon inner knowledge to extend our understanding of the Dreaming. Stanner relates his encounter with Pandak, a member of the Diminin people, towards the end of the old man's life. As a gift to the author he painted a picture of the Dreaming as he saw it. This picture (see Figure 3) gives us a remarkable portrait of 'all the world' as seen by Pandak before he died.

The picture in Figure 3 depicts five strata or empyrean of reality. The topmost stratum reveals four suns which are moving clockwise. The first sun in the left-hand corner is both female and ophitic (relating to the worship of serpents); the second and third suns are male, while the fourth is female, surrounded by clouds. The suns are depicted as nearer the earth than the remote stars, which are again female and unmarried. The second stratum depicts the Milky Way, the third the moon (shown as a cluster of forms between 'new' and 'full'), the planets and the morning star. The planets are male, and the morning star female, with children. The fourth stratum is that of the earth depicted as a steady platform of earth, trees and places near and far. The fifth stratum is the 'within' or the 'underneath' of the earth, through which great (male) stars pass nightly. Finally, each segment of the earth is seen as a distant 'country'.

That the cosmos should be expressed as a quintuple is not so surprising. The legendary 'fifth essence' is said to be the substance of which the heavenly bodies are composed, and is latent in all things. Hence there will always be five aspects inherent in manifestation – that of the four elements of matter and a fifth, the *fiat lux* of the principal of Creation. In the higher empyrean the quaternary of suns representing two male–female pairs is itself a common symbol for the four elements, earth (female), fire (male), air (male) and water (female). The line that links them in Pandak's picture represents the unifying principle that signifies the seminal passage between two 'water suns' (as symbolized by the serpents and clouds) and the central 'male-suns'.

Next comes the empyrean of the Milky Way, regarded by Aborigines as either a creek with stones reflecting in its waters, or a river of the dead where the souls of men return at death.[9] The faint cloudy appearance of the Milky Way is also associated with campfire smoke. Such an image is in accordance with the belief held by many traditional peoples that the Milky Way is the abandoned pathway of the sun or the tracks of gods.[10] Its Elysian connotations are fully

Fig. 3   The Cosmos according to Pandak. Note the five levels of the empyrean as he envisioned them.

authenticated in numerous traditions, making it a powerful symbol of the Abode of the Blessed for all.

In the third empyrean Pandak portrays the lunar phases in conjunction with the planets (all male) and the morning star with her children. In traditional astrology the planets were nearly always anthropomorphized as men, while the morning star (Venus) as a goddess we know was 'born from the sea'. Her 'fructifying waters' are in keeping with Pandak's image of the morning star in the company of her children, the fruit of her womb. Together with the lunar phases (recalling that among Aborigines the moon was male rather than female) and the masculine planets, linked as they are to the feminine morning star, we have a further echo of the principle of unity–duality as delineated in the first empyrean, among the four suns. Only now cyclic elements of time have been introduced in the form of the lunar phases and the planets themselves, traditionally regarded as 'measurements of time'.[11]

What we have witnessed so far in the transition from the first stratum to the third in Pandak's painting is a movement through the heavens from a point of absolute unity, and therefore an echo of the Divine Principle, towards increasing diversity in the form of the River of Souls (implying birth and death) and the cyclic movement of time, itself contingent to manifestation. The serpentine and cloudy nature of the two female suns working with the solar radiance of the male suns bring about the increasing materialization of the spiritual principle in the world. This Pandak explores in the fourth empyrean where he describes trees, vegetation and hills. This, therefore, reflects the realm of matter, life, the very act of manifestation itself, the world of men and animals. Here the laws of contingency reign. He has completed his description of the origin and development of the universe in the fifth stratum with a reference to 'underworld' matter where those forms as yet unrealized await their opportunity to ascend, along with the 'male' stars of the night when they 'turn the world over'.[12]

Such is the complexity of Pandak's cosmogonic view. For many, of course, his painting would be considered archaic, the product of a mythic way of viewing the world. Like the old Ptolemaic system, it sees the world as central to the schema rather than peripheral to the sun. Attributing gender characteristics to the stars and planets in no way adds to our understanding of the universe. But Pandak would argue that he was exploring a metaphysical model of the heavens. More importantly, perhaps, he was attempting to identify where men fit into the larger picture. By placing mankind in the fourth stratum he was subjecting them to the correct hierarchical displacement that all peoples acknowledge – or did until the Renaissance when man placed himself at the centre of the universe. His painting nevertheless successfully integrates the paradox of unity–duality, under the aegis of cyclic time, as it becomes manifest in the world. The male–female nexus dominates his thinking as it did later generations of philosophers who attempted to define the doctrine of opposites (as in Plato's *The Republic*).

Pandak's painting reflects a deeper order of reality pertaining to the Dreaming than many of the myths about Sky Heroes might suggest. It may be argued that he has attempted to define the Dreaming more succinctly than his forebears could have done. Yet the mythic elements are all there. Separate orders of existence, the gradual movement towards manifestation, the role of formless matter and celestial hierarchies in the scheme of things – all these are present in the forms familiar to Aborigines. From my own experience I have heard Aborigines dispense with mythic interpretation in order to extract the symbolic essence. They are more conscious than most peoples of the importance of esoteric analysis and its pre-eminence over the exoteric elements within a story. But, of course, they will only reveal exoteric aspects of a myth to those who are either uninitiated or strangers. Esoteric information they largely keep to themselves.

## SUPERNATURAL POWER AND THE SNAKE MYTHS

Within this schema, however, the image of the Snake remains. The Rainbow Snake is the principle of manifestation inherent in the conduct of the First Cause. The persona given to this First Cause is, more often than not, vague, shadowy and ill defined. He takes the name of Baiame in the east, Ungud in the northwest, Mangela in the west, Pundjel in the south.

His presence is Olympian, remote from the activities of manifestion, yet nevertheless involved. Woodley King,[13] an elder of the Indjabinda tribe in the Pilbara, informed me that Mangela was the 'First Man' who came down to earth. His appearance was fleeting, more in the nature of a visit. The place where he came to earth is recorded in a mound sacred to the Indjabinda people, known as Kumana Kira. In Woodley's view it was the Rainbow Snake, not Mangela, who 'made the world', though at the instigation of Mangela himself. This would accord with the Gnostic concept of the Snake being 'midway between the Father and Matter.' Mangela is therefore the principal cause of world birth, not its agent.

Clearly, the Rainbow Snake is the generative force in the creation of the world. He is not the sole agent, as is witnessed by the presence of countless Sky Heroes responsible for the formation of tribal country. But he appears in nearly all tribal myths as the one agent capable of making rivers, waterholes or rain. He is an agent of water, a vivifying force which all Aborigines recognize as important to their survival. Today he lives in waterholes or under waterfalls, a constant presence in the lives of everyone, adult or child. His character is profoundly ambivalent, of course, in keeping with his mythic status. As a world-creator he acts as a positive force in men's lives. On the other hand there is a misogynistic element to his character, as exemplified in the Waugeluk Sisters myth from Arnhem Land, where he attacks and eats the daughters of Kunapipi, the fertility-mother. Though this is explained as man's need to possess the creative powers of Kunapipi (and therefore of the woman), eating her offspring is also regarded as the Great Snake's eternal desire to retain these powers unto himself.[14]

The process of world-creation on the part of the Rainbow Snake invariably involves a migration. Among the coastal tribes of the north and west of Australia, and those living within a reasonable distance inland, the Great Snake always arrives 'from the sea'. It may be that his appearance from the ocean is an echo of the first people's arrival from Asia 50,000 years ago. Under the names Bolan, Kunukban, Galaru and Unjuat, he is credited with making a landfall at the time of the Dreaming. Further south, however, at a place known

31

Fig. 4   The Great Snake Jarapiri at Jukuita Cave, Tanami Desert.

as Winbaraku (in Central Australia) a reverse migration is recorded. In this case, Jarapiri, the Great Snake, emerges from the mountain and begins his world-creating journey in a northerly direction, surfacing briefly at Jukuita cave (near Yuendumu, Tanami Desert) before continuing towards Milingimbi, a coastal outpost in Arnhem Land. It would seem that for many of the central tribes the Rainbow Snake's journey is offering them – at least in the form of metaphysical return – a path backwards to their source.

The Kunukban myth provides us with a unique record of the Great Snake's journey at the time of the Dreaming. Coming from the island of Puruyu:nungu:kunian far out in the Timor Sea, Kunukban came ashore at Kunununju (now Wyndham) with the intention of capturing Ekarlarwan, the invisible First Cause, in order to wrestle from him the 'secrets for the people'. These secrets were none other than law, culture, ritual and ceremony; the ingredients most needed to regulate the lives of men. Because Ekarlarwan was invisible, Kunukban found himself chasing after his dog instead. The dog, Djaringin, acted as a decoy, luring Kunukban away from Ekarlarwan. Deliberately tricking Kunukban, the dog made a 'twisty track' all over the country, forcing Kunukban to create landmarks and rivers as he went. These are recorded in numerous myths and legends spanning different tribal territories.

Eventually, it seems, Kunukban was able to corner Ekarlarwan at a place known as Wamburing Knob, deep inland. Here Kunukban camped and made his 'big Sunday' ceremony – that is, the wresting away from Ekarlarwan of his 'secrets'. These secrets, which Kunukban then gave to men, embodied in part a vast amount of esoteric information pertaining to his world-creating journey. But more importantly, by giving men access to Ekarlarwan's knowledge, Kunukban made it possible for men to 'talk back' to Ekarlarwan. This talk-back capacity is symbolized in the sound of the bullroarer which is whirled during important ceremonies. It also suggests that for the first time it was possible for men to enter into a dialogue with Ekarlarwan, something which had not occurred before the Great Snake's intercession. Kunukban then continued on his way, travelling deeper into the hinterland of Australia, disseminating the Law and creating landscapes as he went.

This, of course, annoyed Ekarlarwan, who did not like the idea that his secrets had become 'common knowledge'. He sent an emissary, the butcher bird Jolpol, after Kunukban to take back the secrets. Jolpol caught up with Kunukban at a place known as Parndukarni, where he pretended to woo the Great Snake with sweet talk. He did this by confusing Kunukban as to his gender. Kunukban succumbed to this erstwhile siren, allowing Jolpol to push his head into the campfire in an attempt to burn him to death. Unknown to Jolpol, however, the Great Snake's protector, the storm bird Kurukura, managed to attack the butcher bird and drive him

Fig. 5   Silhouettes of the three animal characters of the legend showing the black head coloration and varying amounts of black body coloration due to burn marks obtained when the black cuckoo saved the black-headed python from being incinerated in a campfire by the butcher bird. (After W. Arndt, in *The Dreaming of Kunukban*.)

A Black-headed python, the victim of the fire episode.

B Black-throated (or pied) butcher bird, the villain of the fire episode.

C Black cuckoo, also known as Koel or storm bird, the heroine of the fire episode.

off. But not without some cost to all concerned. The storm bird was burnt all over by the fire, Jolpol was partially burnt, and Kunukban received burns to his head. This is the reason why the storm bird today is black, the butcher bird is black and white, while the 'friendly' snake, known as the black-headed python, has a black head. They are victims of an epic encounter over the possession of esoteric information said to belong to Ekarlarwan, the principal cause of all existence.

With victory assured, Kunukban, along with his faithful lieutenant Kurukura, then took the Law all over the country, revealing it to the people as they went. More landmarks were completed on their journey inland. At their last camp together they said goodbye, before continuing in separate directions. Kurukura flew towards Tennant Creek where she made her permanent camp in Djun-gurra-gurro spring. Kunukban went straight to Beetaloo lagoon on Newcastle Creek which he entered, never to emerge again. It is said he may have continued underground and come out in the sea on 'the other side', meaning the Gulf of Carpentaria further east.[15]

The world-creating journey of Kunukban is typical of Great Snake myths of the north. While details may vary, river systems differ, and the dramatic circumstances arrange themselves in accordance with local conditions, the essence remains the same. There is an invisible First Cause, the generating principle – in this case Ekarlarwan. His attendant takes the form of a wild dog who acts as a deceiver, trickster or fool. The dog provides the 'veil' behind which the First Cause holds unto itself the principial values. It is the task of the Great Snake to 'move eternally towards the Father and unmoved Matter' in an attempt to extract from the First Cause the ingredients of manifestation, the 'laws' of nature and of man. The Great Snake is protected in turn by a female principle, in this case a storm bird. Together their duality becomes one, and between them they are able to retain the 'secrets' captured from the First Cause. Not even the trickster (butcher bird) is able to regain that which is now 'of the world'.

These are perennial metaphysical arguments behind the act of Creation. They are as much a part of the Western philosophic tradition as they are those of traditional peoples. The difference, of course, is that among Aborigines they have

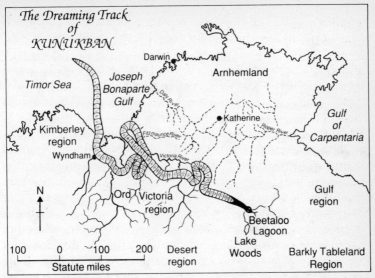

Fig. 6   A map of northwest Australia showing the Ord and
Victoria River Systems (solid lines) relative to other river systems
(dotted lines) and the path or Dreaming track followed by
Kunukban from the Timor Sea to the western fringe of the Barkly
Tableland. (After W. Arndt in *The Dreaming of Kunukban*.)

not been reduced to concepts which appeal to the rational
mind only. Instead they remain in their pristine condition
as living myths. These myths are so fresh that they continue
to retain their vitality for Aborigines today. One observer
remarked how his informant, an elderly Wardaman tribesman,
cried when he discovered a dead black python on the road
one day.[16] This was because the snake represented for him
the presence of the Rainbow Snake, Kunukban. The death of
the biological snake in a sense threatened the eternality of the
Great Snake for the Wardaman tribesman. Nevertheless, what
is interesting in this incident is how the tribesman recognized
in the dead snake on the ground intimations of a metaphysical
order. It is clear that the black-headed python, the butcher bird
and storm bird, not forgetting the trickster dingo, transcend
their organic existence and partake of dramatic events from
the Dreaming each time their paths cross those of Aborigines.
The close proximity of myth and the Sky Heroes in the form

35

of their totemic counterparts clearly make the life of the Spirit such a living event for Aborigines.

According to another report[17] the Rainbow Snake is the ultimate source of a *mekigar* or medicine man's powers (see Chapter 6). The mekigar is 'made' by a fully qualified practitioner who takes the postulant up into the sky by transforming him into a skeleton and placing him in a pouch. He ascends by pulling himself arm-over-arm up the body of the Rainbow Snake until he has reached the sky. There he revives the 'dead' postulant by inserting into him quartz crystals known as *ungur*, yet another name for the Rainbow Snake himself. Thus the postulant rises from the dead through the act of receiving the Rainbow Snake within him in the symbolic form of crystals, the divine scintilla of Ungud himself. In so doing the Rainbow Snake gives the newly made mekigar divine access to the Dreaming from where he ultimately derives his powers.

It is clear from the foregoing material how important the Rainbow Snake is as a spiritual exemplar among Aborigines. He embodies the principle of manifestation and its accompanying laws. The fact that Aborigines receive their own laws as a result of the Great Snake's world-creating activity 'in the world' represents the transition from non-manifestation to manifestation. The Law, so to speak, must be wrestled away from the First Cause (Ekarlarwan/Ungud/Baiame/Mangela) in order that principial unity can achieve material diversity in all the forms of life as we know it. The battle between the two attendants (Jolpol and Kurukura) in the vicinity of primordial fire causes them to be 'disfigured', but it also preserves for all time their living identity in the form of the butcher bird and storm bird. We can see here how a complex metaphysical idea is clothed in the more palpable form of myth, giving it a human dimension in order that it might be understood. One cannot help being reminded in passing of Wittgenstein's dictum which emphasizes the dilemma factual (scientific) interpretation confronts when it successfully answers all possible scientific questions. Under this kind of scrutiny the problems of life remain completely untouched. It is only when the problems 'vanish' – that is become spiritually satisfying in the form of myth – that the problems of life are solved.[18] This suggests that science has no way of answering problems posed by the spirit, however much it might claim to have identified the structure of DNA and the principles of life in the laboratory.

The Rainbow Snake as an expression of world creation resolves that problem. His arrival on the shores of Australia from an unknown source somewhere deep in the ocean suggests that he has come replete with all knowledge. This is true in that he knows how to win for himself (and thus for all men) what the All-father gives up with reluctance. The tension that exists between the Great Snake and the All-father is a necessary but positive tension which ensures that the confrontation between them is heroic, in keeping with the activities expected of Sky Heroes. That their encounter happened during the Dreaming is a sign to Aborigines of the primordiality of world creation, since Ekarlarwan's attempt to escape draws Kunukban ever forward, progressively materializing the landscape as he goes. While the Dreaming might have occurred *then*, its significance is felt *now*. No man can escape the influence of the Dreaming and its accompanying events other than in becoming *dead* to the world. In other words, a non-being. Breaking tribal law can lead to a man being exiled from the world, of course. However, it is a fate no man either seeks or desires. To be condemned in a bone-pointing ceremony for transgressing the law is a fate worse than death because it involves a prolonged psychological collapse that might last for months prior to actual death. Being exiled from contact with the Dreaming by way of ritual and ceremony leaves a man devoid of his own spirituality. He has become dead to the world.

This is the Rainbow Snake's message. He is the most powerful member of the Dreaming pantheon who elicits from lesser Sky Heroes a range of ancillary responses. These in turn become a part of Aboriginal mythology, fleshing out the nuances of meaning inherent in trying to understand the origins of the world. It is this mythology that pervades Aboriginal life throughout the country, making each waterhole and river an echo of his Dreaming presence. It is not possible to travel in the remoter parts of Australia without coming in contact with the Rainbow Snake's *djang* (supernatural power). Each tribe has a compendium of stories relating to his appearance in their country. Many others also have his 'Dreaming-presence' on their cave walls, signifying his timeless appearance in the world. Thus the songs they sing telling of his exploits are a part of his primordial beauty bestowed upon Aborigines 'when the world was young'.

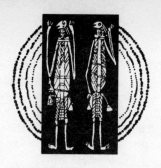

# 3 · TOTEMIC IDENTITY

No other condition more poignantly expresses an Aborigine's relationship with the Dreaming than his totemic identity. For it is the act of identifying with 'something other' than himself that allows a tribesman the opportunity to transcend ordinary reality in an act of union. His totem is both his alter ego and a metaphysical landmark which orients him while he lives. According to Stanner[1] a totem is 'a sign of unity between things or persons *unified by something else*'. Not to have a double or shadow in the world is to be condemned to an inferior existence governed by the here and now rather than by the mysterious plausibilities said to have occurred during the time of the Dreaming. It is this need to be linked to the Dreaming by way of a totem that makes life acceptable, indeed bearable, both in the social as well as the spiritual sense.

Every individual in a tribe is born 'into' a totem. As a result he or she belongs to a group of people, all of whom bear the name of a natural object. The object is usually an animal or plant, but it can also be a natural phenomenon such as water, the sun, cloud or the wind. No aspect of material existence escapes the scope of the totem. All creatures are drawn into its domain, there to link up with a man or woman in order to complete their persona. To deny its existence would lead to a loss of personal identity which would make life intolerable. In contrast, knowing and respecting one's totem ensures that an individual's social identity is preserved. To belong to the possum or emu totem, for example, provides an individual with lifelong social obligations which extend beyond those of his or her immediate family. These in turn ensure continuity and harmony within the tribe.

In a simple tribal structure we are likely to find two or perhaps four classes, of which all tribesmen and women count themselves as members. But within a class they are also members of a totem. In the case of the Urbunna tribe of South Australia the two classes are known as Matthurie and Kirarawa. These in turn possess six totems (*thunthunie*) each, none of which are the same. Thus, in the Matthurie class, we find the following totems: Inyarrie (wild duck), Wutnimmera (green cicada), Matla (dingo), Waragutie (emu), Kalathura (wild turkey), Guti (black swan); while among the Kirarawa we find the Kurara (cloud), Wabma (carpet snake), Kapirie (lace lizard), Urantha (pelican), Kutnichilie (water hen), Wakalia (crow).[2]

In this context a Matthurie man must marry a Kirarawa woman. He cannot marry someone from within his class; nor can she. A further restriction placed upon marriage involves the right 'totemic marriage'. A dingo man (Matthurie) can therefore marry a water hen (Kirarawa); a cicada, a crow; a wild turkey, a cloud; a swan, a pelican and so on. These restrictions are obviously designed to ensure against degradation of the bloodlines through incest. But they do more than that. They ensure that relationships balance one another through the enacting of what one observer[3] regarded as an 'ecological order' in nature itself.

Here we encounter a unique form of identification between men and their natural counterparts. Among the Nunger people of Southwest Australia their two classes are known as the long-billed corella, (*maarnetj-maat*) and the raven (*waardarng-maat*) (The word *maat* means 'a member of'.) To the tribesmen these classes reflect a condition or temperament perceived in nature itself. Thus a long-billed corella is recognized as being a 'getter' (*maarnetj*) because of its food-gathering propensities, and the raven a 'watcher' (*waardarng*) because of its talent for observing. A man, therefore, adopts such a characteristic as soon as he is born into his class and totem.

40

In consequence a 'getter' or active man must marry a 'watcher' or passive woman or vice versa: an 'active' woman must marry a 'passive' man. A further delineation of temperament is also suggested with the prefix 'warm getter' and 'cold watcher'. The Aborigines term these opposing temperaments as 'smart' and 'fool' accordingly.

In the Kimberley region this opposition between 'smart' and 'fool' describes perfectly the temperament of two ground birds, the brolga and the bustard. The brolga is regarded as better, more beautiful and smarter than the bustard which is regarded as stupid, without inventiveness, stubborn, uncontrolled and even reckless. The bustard must always be put in his place by the brolga for his misdeeds. Such characteristics are invariably found among their totemic counterparts. Bustard men or women tend to be plump while brolga men or women have lithe figures. Significantly, only among the larger mammals such as the Kangaroo and dingo, do their temperamental opposites conform to the gender of the same species. A male and female Kangaroo oppose one another as 'active' or 'passive'; so too with the dingo.[4]

Such polar pairings, while they do not happen in nature, nevertheless represent a significant symbolic balancing within the ecological order itself. Animals and birds are opposed one against the other in order to bring about a perceived harmony by neutralizing their contrasting temperaments. In the same way men and women harmonize their own temperaments by way of totemic identification in the form of permitted totemic marriages. This brings about social harmony within the context of the tribe, which in turn makes for long-term stability. Humanizing characteristics perceived in nature set up an 'echo' within the realm of human relationships that does not stray too far from nature itself. In this way totemic identity signifies a reaching out to the world of birds and animals in order to clarify their relationship to man.

Such temperamental parallels extend into the symbolic colour schemes used in body painting at the time of important tribal ceremonies, although these schemes are not consistent throughout Australia. They are, however, consistent within the tribal region. The 'warm and quick' brolga men are identified with the colours red and black; the 'cold and slow' bustard people with the colours yellow and white. Among the 'warm and quick' long-billed corella men and the 'cold and slow' raven people their colours are more apposite. If a man is of the corella class he is classified as 'warm and quick', thereby having a right to the use of red and white in his decorations. His raven counterpart is entitled to the use of black and yellow in his decorations. Black and yellow are therefore slow, 'watcher' colours, while red and white are fast, 'getter' colours.

The colour system extends to a description of the man himself. A corella man is regarded as being fair with a light complexion. He might also be regarded as being as 'clear as water, sweet or pure'. He would be 'demonstrative, well-shaped, with large calves and small ankles', depending on his individual totem. On the other hand, if he were a member of the raven class, he may be described as sturdier or more thickly set, duller or darker in complexion. Essentially, however, his classificatory persona would conform to his 'whiteness' or 'blackness' because of his membership of either the corella or raven class. Subsidiary personal characteristics would derive from his individual totem which may be 'warm and slow' or even 'cold and quick'. The complexity of individual characteristics are therefore easily expressed by way of collective class membership and individual totemic identity. All possible human temperamental variations can be embraced in the act of symbolic identification with nature.

It is a remarkable system. One is tempted to explore totemic identification with nature in the light of its environmental implications. Implicit, of course, in the system is a moral order. At a surface level the contrast between a 'white' and 'black' species tends to degenerate into the battle between good and evil. This is often found in 'just-so' tales such as the battle between the eagle (of the long-billed corella class) and the crow (raven). At a deeper level, such a battle not only identifies the migratory patterns of the birds concerned (they come from different regions of the Southwest), it also suggests a qualititative difference between the two species. The eagle is said to be 'the first of all, the head man,' or 'father of all'. In this sense the eagle transcends his class when he marries, say, a mallee hen, which is forbidden. But, as head man, right or wrong do not apply since Creation is free of morals. The eagle does what he wills in myth. Nevertheless, what is at work here, if in an obscure way, is a form of ecological classification which links all nature into an overall pattern. It is this ecological classification that might bear further investigation in the interest of discovering whether there may be a pairing in nature designed to preserve the balance, and harmony, between species. If this is so, then Aboriginal thought may have provided us with an important new system of classification that can be used as part of environmental protection.

The important aspect of this classificatory system, however, is how it pertains to the social and spiritual life of the Aborigine. Whether he be white or black, quick or slow, smart or foolish, no moral implication should be drawn. It is simply a way of ordering the affairs of men by way of totemic identification. That it might create rivalries at a more mundane level is merely part of the human condition. Excessive rivalry, whether it is intellectual, religious, national or parochial, leads to a degradation of the human condition in the same way as a wrong marriage between two long-beaked corella people or those of the same totem. It is clear that totemic identity is designed to protect Aborigines, who live in small bands anyway, not only from inbreeding but also from allowing too much emphasis being placed upon certain human qualities over those of others. In this way all facets of the human temperament are kept alive, each counterbalancing the other, waxing and waning in accordance with class and totemic marriage.

The origin of totemic identity lies in the Aborigine's understanding of Creation and how men were formed in the first place. Putting aside the mythic presentation of Creation for the moment, one must look at how men and women came into being in the far distant past, or *alchera*. Then, two self-existent beings known as Numbakulla, noticed on the eastern horizon a number of *Inapertwa* or rudimentary human beings who possessed neither limbs nor senses, nor did they eat. Nevertheless, these beings did present the appearance of humanity even if only vaguely. In a sense these Inapertwa represented a transitionary stage in the transformation of animals and plants into men. This condition of shapelessness, when a man is regarded as little more than a small red pebble among many others, is known by the Arunta of Central Australia as *Kuruna*, a term that suggests man's pre-existent form, his archetype. When the Numbakulla completed their transformation, presenting them with their duality as sexual beings, they continued to retain qualities of their earlier existence. This meant that each man and woman was intimately related to his pre-existent form, whether it was flora, fauna or some other natural phenomenon. In the here and now a man or woman cannot discard his or her totem therefore, because to do so is to deny what he or she was at the time of the Dreaming.[5]

This is where totemic identity becomes so complex. A man is both 'himself' in one sense, but is also 'another' in the sense that he participates in an earlier, transitionary form of existence. His totem, whatever it may be, becomes a mirror in which he can see reflected back at him his ideal form prior to its manifestation as himself. This means that embedded in the idea of totemic identity is the primordial encounter between the unmanifest Principle and the realm of manifestation in the mode of duality. A man only becomes 'himself' at the moment when he detaches himself from his ideal state (as a transitional type in the Dreaming) and takes up the garb of conditional existence. Implicit in the concept of totemic identity is this relationship between the transitional type (unburdened with self-consciousness) and the conditional world of mortality and change. The totem, however, acts as an Ariadne's thread, allowing a man to find his way back to his preconscious existence in the Dreaming. He finds himself forever linked to his own origins, both as a spiritual being and as one of nature's manifestations.

It follows that when a man is 'born' into his totem he is initially at least (prior to physical birth), an Inapertwa or the embryo of an ancestral hero. His totemic identity is not given to him through the intercession of either of his biological parents. As we have seen earlier, Aborigines dismiss biological conception in favour of spiritual conception. They are more interested in the spirit-child's entry into the mother as an act of grace. One can't help seeing a distant echo here of the archetype of the Immaculate Conception inherent in

Christianity. In a sense, every Aboriginal woman may be considered a virgin when it comes to receipt of the kuruna within a totemic environment. Whatever sexual encounters she may have had in the past (and these usually commenced at around nine years of age[6]), the entry of a spirit-child into her womb signified the special beneficence of the Sky Heroes towards that woman. Conception is usually precipitated either by a visit to a totem area with a view to becoming pregnant, or by acknowledging that quickening has occurred after a visit to a particular totemic area. Whichever way conception occurs, a woman will always know where it happened, so that the totemic identity of the child is assured.

Totemic identity imposes a variety of taboos upon the individual concerned. He or she is rarely allowed to eat the flesh of his or her totem, and if so only sparingly. Because in doing so a man is eating of himself. As one Aboriginal informant remarked when viewing a kangaroo, 'That one is the same as me', meaning that he and the kangaroo were one. To eat kangaroo meat would therefore be an act of self-denial. The intimate bond between this man and the kangaroo would be broken, thus condemning him to a purgatorial existence outside nature.

It is clear that the relationship between an individual and his totem is not only lifelong, but life-giving. The totem acts as a form of conscience because it identifies an individual with something other than himself or his tribal affiliations. He can speak with his totem, he can revere it, he can even enter into a partnership with it that transcends all other experiences within nature. Furthermore, it grounds him in a spiritual as well as a physical locality – a locality that he identifies as being his 'country'. This implies custodial responsibilities towards his totem area which must be exercised at prescribed ritual moments (see Chapter 4). Knowing his country's songs, knowing how it was created during the Dreaming, knowing the symbols of the body paintings associated with his totem – these are all part of his totemic identity. A man is only a man when he takes on every aspect of his totem. For in doing so he transcends the limitations of himself and enters into a particular category of sacredness.

## CHURINGAS AND SPIRITUAL IDENTITY

This relationship between a man and his totem does, of course, have its symbolic counterpart. The *churinga* embodies his ancestral heritage more completely than any other artefact. Usually made of wood, the churinga is a narrow, oval-shaped artefact said to embody a man's totem. More often than not it has been made by the child's paternal grandfather who has fashioned it from a piece of wood taken from the totem area. The wooden churinga is a personal piece which, in a sense, echoes the existence of a stone churinga held at a totem centre, along with other wooden churingas that have belonged to deceased totem members. The stone churinga is invariably that of the totemic Sky Hero and thus reiterates his timeless presence here on earth.

A churinga is normally presented to an initiate at the time of his circumcision. The formal revelation of his link with the Dreaming ancestors is an important moment in the life of a young man. The mulga wood churinga is passed among the older men, who press it affectionately to their bodies, before handing it on to the initiate. The markings on the board are then explained to the boy, along with the general meaning of complicated chants rendered in a sacred language with which he is unfamiliar. The churinga is rewrapped in leaves, tied with a hair string, and replaced on a platform at the totemic centre. A few yards away, however, lie the stone churinga, said to have been fashioned by the Sky Heroes themselves. The one belonging to the boy's totem is presented by the father to his son who is encouraged to rub his fingers across the sacred markings. After obtaining permission from the Elders present, the father then reveals secret information about his son's totem and the transcendent relationship the son enjoys with his Dreaming counterpart. An Arunta speech of a father to his son recorded earlier this century expresses the importance of such a revelation:

> This is your own body from which you have been reborn.
> It is the true body of the great Tjenterama, the chief of
> the Ilbalintja storehouse. The stones which cover him are

the bodies of the bandicoot-men which once lived at the Ilbalintja Soak [spring]. You are the great Tjenterama himself: today you are learning the truth for the first time. From now on you are the chief of Ilbalintja [the totemic site, i.e. his country, not the tribe's]: all the sacred *churinga* are entrusted to you for safe keeping. Protect them, guard *the home of your fathers* [author's italics], honour the traditions of your people. We will have many things to tell you. More verses, greater and more secret ceremonies will be made known to you than to any of your mates. *They are all your own heritage*: we have only kept them in trust for you. Now we are getting old, and we pass them on to you since you are the chief re-incarnate. Keep them

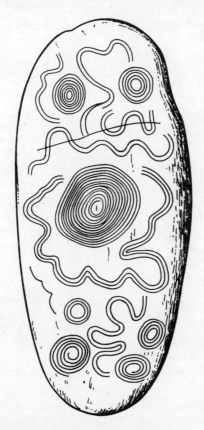

Fig. 7  Inscribed stone churinga, Central Australia.

secret until you are growing old and weak; and then, if
no other young men of the bandicoot totem are living, pass
them on to other tried men from our clan who may keep
alive the traditions of our forefathers until another chief
be born.[7]

Clearly this speech reflects how important the transmission of
esoteric information is in the life of the Aborigine. The initiate
is made privy to sacred knowledge which belongs to him by
birthright. As a member of the bandicoot totem he is receiving
unto himself totemic information that has been a part of tribal
religious history since the time of the Dreaming. In the act of
touching his stone churinga for the first time, and learning
the chants of his totem, an initiate takes possession of his
spiritual persona. He is no longer living a half life in the here
and now, but has been invited to participate in a transcendent
existence by way of his totemic past. From this moment on
his metaphysical heritage becomes paramount. He cannot live
apart, nor does he wish to, from the exigencies of his totemic
origins. It follows, then, that the bandicoot is no longer a mere
animal that inhabits his landscape, but a continual reminder
of his other existence as a spiritual being.

As it is now evident, reincarnation plays a significant role
in Aboriginal totemic belief. A man (or woman) is never so
uniquely himself that he is not the reincarnation of someone
else. In addition the idea that he might be the reincarnation
of a Sky Hero places him in an unusual position in that he
is the living embodiment of an Alcheringa ancestor and, as
such, is always held in high regard by his tribe. The rebirth
of a totemic hero ensures that the Dreaming is never a faraway
event in the minds of an Aborigine. His very presence, both
as himself and as something 'other' makes him a person to be
venerated. Not all men are reincarnated Sky Heroes, only those
who appear to possess special qualities which his confrères
regard with special affection. These qualities usually set him
apart as someone to be respected, a totemic leader who will
lead the chants, perform the rituals, and become, in time, the
custodian of esoteric lore.

Totemic identity does not end with one's personal totem,
however. A man also adopts those of his father, and treats
his father's churinga as his own after the latter's death.

This adoptive relationship to a father's totem flies in the face of the perceived uninvolvement of the father in his son's conception. The son will receive and learn the sacred lore pertaining to the father's totem before he dies, in much the same way as the son received this information from the Elders at his personal totemic site. He also becomes a guardian to his father's churinga, and even identifies with certain characteristics that might be associated with his father's totem. An Arunta man once reported that the reason why he limped was because his father's totem (or at least his father's father's), was the kangaroo whose leg had been broken at the time of the Dreaming. Thus, on the death of his own father, the Arunta man walked with a limp in sympathy with his father's father's totem. Another man confirmed that he knew his father's chants as if they were his own. He further remarked that his father's churinga and his own churinga were one and the same thing.[8]

Totemic identity is not only a transcendent bond that binds one man to another, or a man to his Dreaming ancestor, it also draws him into a custodial role when it comes to spiritual information. He becomes, in a sense, the inheritor of all that is most relevant in a man's life. With little sense of ownership pertaining to objects of utility or value, he is nevertheless acutely aware of his custodial responsibilities in the context of metaphysical information. Such details cannot be shared with others except under ritual circumstances. Nor can this knowledge be owned by another except when it is 'given'. For a man to take possession of certain ritual information – songs and chants, or even dances, – that does not belong to him by totemic right is seen as a grave crime by Aborigines. He is liable to severe punishment, even exile, for engaging in such antisocial acts. The knowledge he has stolen cannot belong to him because it is rooted in a totemic area, not in any separate intellectual conceit determined by the perpetrator.

On the whole, the Sky Heroes determine in whom they shall manifest themselves according to clan and totemic necessity. But on occasions, it seems, even they make mistakes, reincarnating themselves in the wrong people in the wrong places. This can lead to the loss of totemic identity in the living which results in social disruption and personal suffering. Such accidents usually occur when a woman is visiting neigbours for an extended period of time, or when she is attending lengthy ceremonies on an *inkura* or sacred ground (considered neutral), and is therefore not in her own country. When conception occurs under such circumstances and a child is born, he must go through many trials before he is able to claim his personal churinga later in life. Obviously his own totemic clan do not wish to see him quit his home among them for that of strangers. Often proof of totemic identity can prove to be equally difficult to obtain. If the churinga of his totem has been stolen, or lent out to others and not returned, it makes the task of proving his totemic identity that much harder. Until he finds his churinga and so confirms his totemic identity, a man finds himself living in limbo, his persona incomplete, and liable to derision by those around him. Such a loss of identity can cause grave suffering and contribute further to tribal tensions. A totemic alien in their midst does not make for smooth functioning of the ceremonies, after all.

Such an occasion was recorded by Strehlow when he met a man who had been conceived on the Rara-rara plain (in Central Australia) while his mother was visiting a neighbouring locality. The boy later underwent all his initiation rites at the home of his father at a different locality. He was accepted as a member of the bandicoot totem by his own male relatives. After he had grown up he found it difficult to visit his birthplace on Rara-rara plain because the area then belonged to white settlers. Ceremonial gatherings there became infrequent. It was not until he was forty, when the trustees of the area where his mother had conceived him revealed the Rara-rara ceremonies to him in Alice Springs one day, that he was able to claim them as their rightful heir. It appeared that until this point he had been too shy to enter the strange territory of the neighbouring tribe who had been guarding the churinga on his behalf! As a result he regretfully confessed to Strehlow, 'I am altogether ignorant of my own home. I have never heard its legends or its chants. I have never seen it [his country] or witnessed its ceremonies.'[9] One wonders to what extent this man felt the loss of such important religious and cultural artefacts during the early part of his life. It seems that he would have been condemned to a life of spiritual ignorance had not his real totemic clansmen saved him.

It is clear that the possession of a totem forms a vital part of an Aborigine's perception of himself and his relation to the world. He is not content merely to accept the world as it is, in spite of his seeming lack of concern for individual destiny. Totemic identity signifies a spiritual link with ancestral activity at the time of the Dreaming. Furthermore, it extends his persona far beyond that of the conventional ego into a realm which partakes of the divine. Its stone or wooden counterpart, known as the churinga, is a symbolic expression, an icon, that affirms this unique relationship for the duration not only of his physical existence, but also of his spiritual existence. In a sense, the totem offers the Aborigine a chance to step outside time, even if time only exists for him in its cyclic mode. The churinga storehouse located at a totem centre houses the individual churinga of all his forebears, making it possible for him to share with them their past lives. In this way he is able to dismiss death as a partial reality only. In taking possession of his churinga, learning the songs, dances and chants that make up his totemic repertoire, he is taking into himself a level of reality that subsumes all others. This is why he can say, as one informant remarked, 'Sea-eagle and me, we one body.'[10] Or as another said, 'My totem and me, we're the same.' In other words, a man of the bandicoot totem and the animal in question are actually brothers.[11]

When one compares this mode of thought to the one expressed earlier in the chapter pertaining to ecological ordering within nature, one begins to sense a dimension of experience which is entirety outside conventional cognitive processes as we know them in the West. It is with some reluctance that one would wish to term these 'prehistoric' since to do so places them at the onset of some evolutionary model. The truth is that totemic identity exists today among Aborigines who have long been in contact with Western thought, religion and ethics. Yet they refuse to discard their need for a totem, thus affirming a ritual, esoteric and emotional link with their country that helps them to reject European property laws and the rights of ownership these imply. The Aborigines' 'property laws' as such are of a more transcendent order, capable of embracing psychic and spiritual terrain far in excess of any based upon observable data. The totem is the man, and the man is his totem. Perhaps this form of self-identification is in keeping with an older, more pristine awareness of the interrelatedness of everything in nature. It is an awareness that may well be in need of revival if we are to begin to establish a true understanding of the earth upon which we live before it is too late. Indeed totemic identity may be our last opportunity to rectify the abuses we have subjected nature to in the past 100 years. In the words of an anonymous Latin writer, 'Man commands nature by obeying her.'[12] Relating to one's totem may well be the only way left to develop a new reverence for what may be termed Earth wisdom.

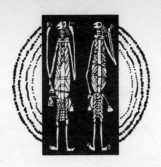

# 4 · RITE AND RITUAL

Few people in the world are so dominated by their ritual life as the Aborigines. Their vast history has left them with a ceremonial legacy that extends into almost every aspect of existence. So pervasive is this legacy, it would be true to say that Aborigines are unable to alter the course of their lives because of it. Rite and ritual govern all transitions, whether they be those of birth, adolescence, adulthood or crossing the border into death. Their ancestors have devised ceremonies which circumscribe social relationships, marriage, even sexual behaviour. The world of the Aborigine is a complex calendar of events spanning his entire existence on earth to the point where he rarely acts outside the aegis of tribal law when it comes to asserting his individuality.

This is not to say that the Aborigine is passive in his encounter with the world. But what it does mean is that he has fixed, time-honoured models by which he can understand reality and so respond to it in a fashion that causes the least disruption to those around him. The concept of individualism is largely alien to him, yet equally he feels no compunction about asserting his identity within the context of ritual existence. The world of his totem ensures him a place not only as a ceremonial exemplar, but also as someone who partakes of dual identities. Therefore he is able to express himself in terms of his totem while remaining a member of a society whose relationships are often more highly structured than those in a play.

This is not to suggest that Aborigines resent their reliance on the ceremonial pageant. Rather, the opposite is true: they regard ritual as a complement to living, as it allows them to partake of a more metaphysical dimension in contrast to their day-to-day activities. Wedded to nature and the business of finding enough food each day, Aborigines are at pains to find meaning in such mundane events, if only to justify the singularity of their lives. The land, its creation at the time of the Dreaming, the mysterious workings of the Sky Heroes, and the civilizing effect of tribal law all require formal acknowledgement by way of rite and ritual, song and ceremony if men are to understand why they are here in the first place. A dance, the secret words of a chant – such things merely emphasize the closeness of the other world, the Alcheringa, when the immortal coils of Creation were first determined.

The etymology of the word 'rite' more properly suggests the origin of Aboriginal ceremony than does its obvious association with religious ritual. This, of course, is never far away, as most ceremonies are in one way or another religious. But the earlier etymological meaning, deriving from the Latin word *recte* meaning 'in a straight line, perpendicularity, uprightly' goes nearer to the heart of what Aboriginal ritual means to them. The idea of proceeding 'upwards' is inherent in most rituals, since most of them derive their origin from the Sky Heroes themselves. Cultural heroes traversed all of the country at the time of the Dreaming, bestowing upon the First People as they did their knowledge of custom and law. It follows that any ritual enacted in memory of these events necessarily inclines the participants 'upwards' towards the 'big fella, number one' in the sky. This may be Ungud, Numbakela, Mangela or Baiame, it does not matter. The important thing is that Aborigines feel themselves ascend from a mundane to a supramundane condition whenever they perform their rites.

## INITIATION RITES

The idea of blood-letting or blood sacrifice is rooted in Aboriginal ritual practice. There are few ceremonies that do not involve the cutting of some part of the body in order to release blood. Even for more practical purposes such as requiring an adhesive substance for sticking feather down on their bodies in preparation for a ceremony, cutting a vein and allowing blood to drip into a bowl is a necessary act. But it is as a basis for the ceremony itself that blood sacrifice finds its true resonation. It is not until a man (or woman) has encountered pain by way of a ritual cut that he (or she) enters into the full experience of being considered a social entity, and therefore 'alive'. In the strict sense a boy cannot become a man until he has undergone initiation. Until he is initiated, it follows that he lives only a part life as a child. Ritual initiation allows him to be 'reborn' into a more complete life as an adult.

Prior to European contact young girls often underwent ritual deflowering by men of the same class as the intended husband. This also involved a clitoral cut with a stone knife, followed by intercourse with the men concerned. The girl's head was then decorated with headbands made from bandicoot fur, her neck with necklaces, her arms with fur string, and her body with a mixture of fat and red ochre.[1] Later she was handed over to her husband who might allow the men one more right of intercourse with her before she became forbidden to them. As the girl is around fourteen or fifteen at this stage, it is unlikely that she is a virgin. Normal sexual contacts would have already been made with young boys in their adolescent phase, so that her ritual defloration would be less traumatic than it appears at first sight. What is important here is that the young woman passes from indiscriminate sexual contact outside her prescribed class affiliations into the more rigid mores associated with class membership. The young woman now has obligations, sexual and otherwise, which make her an upholder of collective cultural identity. She has become a woman and is no longer a flagrant sexual vehicle for others.

In the case of the young boy, his initiation also involves blood sacrifice in the form of circumcision, and sometimes even subincision (that is, the splitting of the head of the penis).

Prior to the former event, however, the boy is usually subject to a tossing rite (*alchirokiwuma*, from *alchira* the sky, and *iwuma* to throw) which involves throwing him in the air. While the men are doing just that, the women gather about and call out '*Pau, pau-a-a!*' Then the boy's chest and back are painted with emblems pertaining to various totems, or rock painting designs, though these are not necessarily those of his own totem. The design is called *enchichichika* and, along with the tossing ceremony, is said to promote growth into manhood. The boys are asked to remove themselves from the women's camp and join the men in theirs. From this point on they are expected to join the men on the hunt, abstain from playing with girls, not eat certain foods and to allow their nose to be pierced. All these new directives further prepare the boys for manhood just as throwing them into the sky affirms 'where they have come from' in a ritual act.[2]

It is the second ceremony or *lartna*, however, where a young man is fully initiated into the tribe. Such a ceremony involves all the young boys who have reached puberty or beyond, and occurs, at least in the Central Desert region, on an *apulla* ground. The ceremonial ground has a pathway cleared between two heaped-up mounds, reaching some forty feet in an east–west direction. The symbolic significance is obvious: the pathway from sunrise to sunset further emphasizes the passage of a man's life as it echoes the movement of the sun through the heavens. It is at this point that the boy must shed blood in order to earn his manhood. In the act of circumcision a boy's potency is circumscribed in a ritual act designed to invest him as a 'risen sun' with the power to bestow new life on the tribe. The sun as a seminal agent is thus linked to the boy's life by way of the new corona of flesh on his penis, caused by the circumcisionary wound. From now on he must see himself as reborn in the same way as the sun is reborn each morning.

During the ceremony a boy's personality undergoes an abrupt and permanent change. Not only must he experience pain in the act of submission to his Elders, he must also learn obedience. From being an unruly child, immune to discipline and often unruly in his behaviour, suddenly he becomes someone who implicitly acknowledges the authority of his

Elders. Sworn to secrecy about the rites he has witnessed, the initiate finds himself transformed by the nature of his experience into a man on whom the burden of cultural continuity is already beginning to fall. Though circumcision and subincision are blood rites in the strict sense, they are also transformation rites in another, For it is only by shedding blood, by experiencing ritualized pain, that a man's capacity for reflection (self-awareness) begins to blossom. It is not until he is wounded by his own kind does he recognize that his penchant for self-destruction (through lack of self-discipline) can be a threat to his tribe's well-being. Initiation circumscribes his youthful anarchy once and for all, paving the way for the initiate to become a useful member of his tribe.

As a *rukuta* or novice, the young man is subject to three or more days of varied emotions. For the first time in his life he experiences real fear, exhilaration, uncertainty, and sometimes pride. The Elders press home their advantage as teachers and culture-bearers, drawing him into their circle of knowledge. He must learn a secret language (*ankatja kerintja*) and address all men he chances to meet in this language. He also must learn a collection of chants which have been set apart as the property of the rukuta. These chants are normally associated with particular myths, and with natural phenomena intrinsic to their homeland. As one informant remarked:

> The old men first taught us the verses relating to the Jutalbma, the high mountain, where the rukuta men assembled. We had to sing of the mountain, and of the wallabies which played in the caves on its slopes. We had to learn the verses describing sunrise as seen from the high mountain. It is heralded by the singing of birds at grey dawn. Then comes the flush of the sky in the east; and finally the first rays of the sun lights up the tips of the spinifex grass on the mountain . . .
>
> All those rukuta who had learnt their verses industriously, and who had obeyed their overseer in all things as their duty demanded, received a reward: they were taught the last and most secret verse of this aroa [rock wallaby] chant, the verse containing the name of the blind aroa Father himself. The old men kept this secret to the very last. Only a good and industrious novice may be entrusted with it, not a rukuta whose thoughts are always occupied with women.[3]

It is clear from this explanation that esoteric information is passed on to the novice for the first time in his life. He is privy to secrets upon which his entire tribal culture is based. The gift of a personal bullroarer at this point further emphasizes the new-found 'language of the gods' that the boy now possesses. He is informed that the noise of the bullroarer is the voice of the Sky Heroes talking to him. He is told to whirl the boomerang as often as he wants, thus encouraging him to enter into an interior dialogue with his ancestral heroes.

One can only imagine how a novice must be feeling about these painful changes at this point. The world of his childhood has been ceremonially severed from the rest of him. Circumcision reveals a new dimension to his psyche. He has entered the company of men and there is obviously a rich collusion between them and the Sky Heroes. What they know, what they teach him is of a different order of reality. Powerless, and unable to escape his peers, the novice is made aware that only now is he emerging from an inferior condition – that of unreflective childhood. From now on he must acknowledge as supreme the mysterious world of the Dreaming from which all things flow. His new status entitles him to further instruction into the secret life of the tribe. Totem dances are performed by the Elders, songs are sung, and totemic body paintings are revealed to him for the first time. Through witnessing these ceremonies his one-dimensional soul acquires depth, and in the process he is reduced to silence. For it is only in silence that a boy can become a man.

Final citizenship, however, is not bestowed upon a novice until he has passed through the inkura ceremony some time later. Now known as an *iliara* the novice, along with his friends, are brought to a prepared clearing in which a long mound of earth has been raised. This is where the boys will sleep, their heads resting against the earth mound for the period of the ceremonies. Fires nearby keep them warm at night, and in the morning their ashes are strewn on top of the sacred mound. While the mound remains in the clearing, no man dares to leave. To quit the inkura ground unannounced would be to invite sickness or even death upon those who had proved unequal to the task.

Each iliara receives a new churinga or bullroarer, decorated with the traditional patterns of his totem. Throughout the night they are encouraged to whirl them. Even in sleep an iliara finds himself subject to the sound of the bullroarers, this time whirled by the Elders who wish to wake him and his comrades for further instruction. The fully initiated young men assemble in front of their Elders who then nominate a ceremony in which they are invited to participate. For the first time some of the iliara are asked to provide blood for the decorative body patterns which are placed on their comrades by the elder men. In this way the sacred designs are passed on to the younger generation. Soon everyone is ready to perform their first inkura dance under the guidance of one of the older men. By dawn, after some hours of dancing, the iliara are ready to go out hunting in order to place meat offerings at the feet of the Elders when they return – as a sign of their obedience and thanks. In the days following the young men learn more dances, are taught new chants, and undergo further privations in the form of lack of sleep and food. As one informant explained:

> We used to wait wearily, our stomachs aching from hunger. We did not dare to approach too closely before we had been called. We lived in great terror of our fathers when they were assembled on the inkura ground. At last they would call us. We used to run forward, lay the killed game at the feet of the chief, and join in the dance. Our Elders roasted the meat. We would see, from the down still adhering to their bodies, that they had been engaged in other ceremonies during our absence. We said: 'They must have fashioned great churinga today.' They would not show them to us; *we could not bear their power* [author's italics]. We did not dare to question our fathers: our fear was too great.[4]

Ceremonies such as these, accompanied as they were by strict fasting and sleeplessness, were designed to make the iliara even more subservient to the will of their Elders. In becoming so, they were made more amenable to the transmission of esoteric information vital to the spiritual well-being of the tribe. Blood and food offerings, encounters with their totemic ancestors by way of the songs and dances, these all combined to transform the psychic terrain of the iliara so that they could experience and understand personally the intense spiritual reality inherent in the revelation of the Alcheringa. What previously they might have regarded as 'old men's stuff' was now a part of their own heritage as fully initiated men. The 'architecture of the soul' as Weil termed such spiritual knowledge, had been put in place so that the iliara might themselves contribute to cultural continuity as they grew older.

Initiation, therefore, represents an important point of transition to a more metaphysical world-view for the Aborigines. Conventional terms such as 'rite of passage' often obscure the underlying need for such people to affirm the right of transcendence that is available to all men on attainment of their majority. Blood rites may seem cruel adjuncts to the process, but in reality they are part of the movement away from youth into adulthood. A man must learn to suffer if he is to become a reflective being capable of contributing to social cohesion. Knowing pain is to experience the metaphor of evil by discarding the 'old life', represented by the foreskin, in favour of the new. It is not something that can simply be explained as we might do in our own society. Becoming a man involves crossing over a Rubicon of sorts – a line that marks the beginning of a soul-life as distinct from creaturely existence. In comparison, childhood is creature existence because it involves little more than acceptance. Whereas becoming a fully initiated man marks him as someone who has consented to the journey that life offers. His goal now is to reach his destination using all the cultural criteria handed on to him by his Elders.

It is interesting to note that the word iliara (Strehlow) or urliara (Spencer and Gillen) means a 'perfectly developed member of the tribe'. The word itself is derived from ura, meaning fire. Thus a man who has undergone various tests during the inkura round of ceremonies is someone who has been made perfect by fire, or someone who has received fire into himself. (Hence the significance of ashes strewn over the headrest of the iliara.) According to one informant, the inkura ceremony is designed to strengthen all who pass through it. It imparts wisdom, makes a man more kindly natured and less apt to quarrel. In other words, it makes a man *ertwa murra oknirra* or 'a very good man.' The moral imperatives are so strongly emphasized that it is hard to see someone not being changed by his experiences. Is it any wonder then that various initiatory phases entered into throughout a man's life inevitably entitle him to be known by various status names. But only as an iliara is he considered to be a 'perfect man.'[5]

## THE ROLE OF ART IN RITUAL

In a sense, all ceremonies are initiatory ceremonies. The elaborate world of totems, with their complex body emblems and accompanying songs and dances – these, too, fulfil initiatory functions whenever they are performed. For they bring men in contact with the dual aspect of themselves, that part of which can only be approached by way of metaphor, visual or otherwise. The role of art in this activity is vital. Whether it is the careful incisions made on a churinga or the often elegant symbolism of a body painting – or indeed the elaborately rendered image on a cave wall depicting a Sky Hero such as the Wandjina[6] – few will deny that the Aborigines have developed an iconography capable of rendering their most profound beliefs. All art becomes an integral part of ritual and ceremony, and is rarely detached from these except where European influence has been brought to bear. Recent art movements in Central and Northern Australia are a product of such encounters. What was once sacred, and sometimes secret, is steadily being eroded by economic pressures fuelled from outside these communities in order to satisfy spiritual cravings elsewhere in the world.

Aboriginal art is one of the few genuinely religious arts left in the world. Throughout Australia there is a vast network of caves and rock outcrops on which this art is expressed. To travel the country in search of these 'open-air cathedrals'[7] is to encounter a primeval panorama of grace. Whether it is the Lightning Brothers near Katherine, the Wandjina of the Kimberley, the Quinkin men of Cape York or the Great Snake motif at Ngama, in the Central Desert region, one is immediately struck by the dignity of these paintings. To see them solely as works of art is to diminish their importance to Aborigines. They are more like altar pieces, meditational aids, numinous icons. I recall an encounter with Jarapiri, the

Great Snake, at Ngama some years ago, in the company of its custodians. It was clear when the old men approached the painting that it was not a painting at all. Passing their hands along its entire length, they invoked Jarapiri whom they firmly believed 'made the painting' by entering the cave wall. As far as these Walbiri tribesmen were concerned, Jarapiri was not an ochred reflection of their spirit-being, but a ritual embodiment of the Great Snake itself.[8]

Art is a ritual encounter with the Dreaming. Each cave painting, for example, is cared for by its traditional owners, men known as 'keymen' because they are responsible for their protection and upkeep. Many of the rock paintings are located in important ceremonial sites, and are visited at regular intervals. West of Katherine, the Lightning Brothers, Yagjagbula and Jabiringi, are the centre of rainmaking rituals prior to the end of each dry season. Until recently the Wardaman people used to gather below the rock face each year to perform ceremonies and dances. Even today their custodian, Idumdum (Bill Harney, a Wardaman tribesman), knows all the stories associated with the brothers. Equally, Larry Tchakamurra is familiar with the songs and chants belonging to Jarapiri at Ngama.

Nevertheless, it is interesting to follow the course of image creation. In my journeys I have often asked myself how and why a particular spirit takes the form it does. The Wandjina of the Kimberley are luminous figures of a high order, entirely unlike any others in Australia. Why did they take on their peculiar ghost-like countenance, with their large eyes and no mouth? The answer came by way of one of their custodians, David Mowaljarlai, a Naringin tribesman.

According to Mowaljarlai, the Wandjina do not take their form from rain-bearing clouds, as was suggested by some observers, but from a natural artefact lying hidden in the body of a long-necked turtle. In fact, the Wandjina's form is modelled on the gullet and neck bones of this turtle. Mowaljarlai insists that the Wandjina 'puts his image in his chosen animal,'[9] in this case, the sweetwater turtle. In the same way as a spirit-child enters a woman's womb at an *ungud* (sacred) place in nature, the Wandjina enters his chosen form in order to become 'born into the world'. He further insists that the sweetwater turtle 'holds the image of Man' in its breast. In every sweetwater turtle lies a reminder of the 'Creation of Man'.

The origin of a sacred image being derived from nature is further enhanced by the story of Kunukban, the Rainbow Snake's, creation at the time of the Dreaming. (see Chapter 2, p.31.) According to Kulumput, a Wardaman Elder,[10] Kunukban derived its form from the black-headed python, even though he acknowledged that the Great Snake originally arrived in Australia from the island of Puruyu:nungu:kunian, far out at sea. Presumably at this point the Great Snake had no manifest form since he acquired his particular image after he was attacked by Jolpol, the butcher bird. During the fight Kunukban was dragged into a fire, while his own protector, the storm bird Kurukuru, fought to save his life. In the resulting fracas Kunukban's head was burnt, Kurukuru received burns all over his body, and Jolpol received minor burns to his head and wings. These body markings reflect the visible presence of the black-headed python, the black-throated, or pied, butcher bird, and the black cuckoo or storm bird today.

Kunukban, the Rainbow Snake and the Wandjina derive their visible form from nature, so that what happens in the process of deification is of another order. The Aborigines recognize that the natural object is capable of being imbued with supernatural power (djang, ungud, kurunba), thus raising it to another level of experience. The process of rendering the image as art in part defies man's ability to do so. Often an Elder will explain that a rock painting was not put there by men, but by the Spirit itself. The idea that a sacred image might 'not be made by men's hands' (acheiropoietos) is not uncommon among major spiritual traditions. It is said that Christ miraculously imprinted His image on the Mandilion, a piece of fabric conveyed by messengers to Abgar, the King of Edessa, when he asked Him for His portrait. This portrait was preserved in Constantinople until it disappeared during the time of the Latin occupation.[11] The ritual aspect of retouching a painting is no more than a practical adjunct to the original creation at the time of the Dreaming. Aborigines acknowledge that the Spirit resides in the rock, and it is only its image that they are renewing.

Knowing that a sacred portrait was not made by human hands lends distinct authority to any rock painting. In this respect Aborigines are endowed with a level of perception which transcends so-called objective reality. It is a perception that most traditional peoples resort to when they wish to explain metaphysical phenomena. While at one level they see with their eyes; at another, they 'see' with their intellect only. It is this kind of intellectual perception that was first identified by Gregory of Palamas, an Orthodox theologian of the fourteenth century. He spoke of uncreated light, or 'immaterial Light' – a substance, not an energy – which permeated the world of sensible images when they had been deified. Therefore it was not a material light which shone upon the apostles on Mount Tabor, but something suprasensible which belonged to the 'supernatural world of grace'.[12] While the distance that separates an Aboriginal custodian and an orthodox theologian may seem great, they do appear to agree on one point: the existence of uncreated and unlimited divine power (energy). Palamas calls this energy a 'deifying energy' which 'deifies those who partake of it'. The Aborigines speak of it as *djang* or *ungud*, the supernatural power which permeates any sacred place or object. Aborigines are quick to apply the term to what they feel with their hearts and minds whenever they approach a cave painting. What they are experiencing can only be isolated by way of ritual and ceremony, and so given form in their minds.

Ritual art extends into a number of other areas. In pre-European contact days, and well into this century, Aborigines regularly painted ceremonial mounds prior to an important ritual. For the duration of the ceremonies such a mound would embody djang, signifying that the spirit of the Alcheringa had entered it. When the ceremonies were concluded the painting was either destroyed or the clearing abandoned until the Alcheringa spirits were deemed to have left the place. In this way the dignity of the painting was always preserved. Such dignity was also associated with mortuary painting, a painting that has achieved its most distinct expression among the Tiwi people from Bathurst Island off the Northern Territory coast. These people continue to daub their death poles (*pukamani*) with complex designs pertaining to the totemic identity of the deceased. His 'other' life is therefore preserved as a living reminder of his metaphysical existence.

Perhaps this is why Aborigines never indulged in portraiture. Their metaphysical and tribal identity seemed to preclude any need to identify their personal characteristics. Even modern painters rarely personalize their work, whether it is in a traditional format or on canvas as fine art. It is as if the Aborigine has allowed his personality to be subsumed by what Shi'ite theologians call 'Qualities of Action'.[13] This is the only way whereby a man can express himself, not in visible portraiture which cannot capture his essence. A man's totemic identity is therefore a closer rendition of his true persona, and therefore capable of expression in body painting, on mortuary artefacts or as a Dreaming.

A man's Dreaming is all that a man owns. It is a metaphysical possession linked to the place where he was conceived. In a sense, it is a concept of origin which a man possesses from the moment he is born. No one can dispossess him of his Dreaming, nor can anyone paint it without his permission. Such a Dreaming is ritually revealed to a man during initiation ceremonies. Prior to this he owns his Dreaming unconsciously, without being privy to its esoteric significance. But once these have been revealed to him he is entitled to express his Dreaming only at ritually prescribed times. Thus his true identity is made up of a combination of his totem and his country which are all derived from his place of conception. It is not possible to detach these from the man (or woman). Only in the present day has this custom changed. Now many artists paint their Dreaming and sell them through commercial art galleries. The esoteric aspects of their Dreaming, however, are usually left out of the paintings. In this way their secret, metaphysical identity is preserved.

Rite and ritual are essential to the realization of being among Aborigines. Without their ceremonies, their ritual chants and songs, their totemic dances, these people would be deprived of their ability to survive. They know, for example, that not to perform ceremonies inevitably results in a decline in the power of nature to renew itself. They believe all nature relies on them to renew its life force through the performance of rites.

It is widely believed (and clearly evident to the eye) that when ceremonies are no longer performed in certain regions, the animals and birds soon leave. So that rites are, in a sense, an embrace between man and nature. It is the only way in which man can converse with nature on an equal footing. When he is cloaked in the mantle of ceremony, then an Aborigine feels he is fully in accord with the universe, and that nature and he are one. Indeed, it is perhaps uniquely Aboriginal to say he sees himself not as separate from nature, but that he and nature are bondsmen.

It is a subject that bears further discussion. Can one say that the diminishing role of nature as a partner in the creation of the world has been brought on by the decline of ritual in modern life? Modern science has placed us in the position where man has, to some extent, control over nature. In so doing we have learnt to manipulate it, causing in the process untold environmental damage. The animals are disappearing, countless species are becoming extinct each year. Without the benefit of ritual or, of a metaphysical double in the form of a totem, we have no way of restraining our penchant for exploitation. We acknowledge no taboos, nor restrictions on how we might utilize nature. It is this kind of Earth wisdom which modern man has all but lost. It seems that the Aborigines, together with other traditional peoples throughout the world, are the only ones with the understanding to arrest the forces of destruction that we have unleashed upon the planet. It appears that this form of religious ritual is the metaphysical key with which we might unlock a door that has been closed to us for too long. If we do not use it, we may well find ourselves unable to influence a process that is already taking us along the road to destruction.

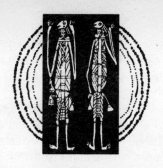

# 5 · THE ART OF MYTH

Maurice Bowra described myth as 'a story whose primary purpose is not to entertain but to enlighten'.[1] He further went on to suggest that myths are not created in a rational spirit of explanation but appeal to half conscious elements within human nature. Bowra suggested that prehistoric man had little power of analysis or abstraction, nor did he have the linguistic or mental resources required for analytical thought. Such a perception is typical of an intellectual standpoint which sees myth as an archaic form of reasoning entirely divorced from the metaphysical dimension it wishes to explore.[2] Yet among Aborigines myth is as genuine a form of metaphysical expression as Aquinas's *Summa Theologica* was to medieval Christians.

It comes as no surprise, then, that throughout Aboriginal Australia there is a vast body of oral literature pertaining to the origin and creation of the world, the nature of the Dreaming, the birth of social institutions and spiritual law, how tools and artefacts came into existence, and how nature fits into the overall mosaic. To argue that such myths and legends merely obscure the intellectual process misses the point. Myth is a way of attaching deeper psychological meaning to the principle of intellectual understanding, whereby such things as modes of behaviour, new discoveries and metaphysical insights themselves are successfully integrated into the overall pattern of existence. In other words, myth is not a reflection of archaic consciousness but a canny device used by most oral cultures to imbue their perceptions with real significance.

A language of myth enables the Aborigines to define a complex range of beliefs which otherwise might go unnoticed. The truth is that the range of Aboriginal languages (there are, or were, over 500 distinct languages, including dialects, spoken by Aborigines at the time of European contact[3]) made for a diverse collection of myths. Contrary to popular belief, Aboriginal languages are extremely complex in their syntax and grammar, which in itself ensured that most ideas could be explored by them. Since European contact, however, Pidgin has become the lingua franca among most Aboriginal tribes, resulting in a subsequent decline in intellectual insights, due to the reduced number of words available. Further- more, Pidgin is essentially a practical language devised for communication with their European overlords. It has none of the linguistic subtlety of indigenous languages, and so is a poor vehicle for expressing the old myths with which earlier generations were so familiar. It is not surprising, then, to discover that many of the earlier myths have been lost simply because there are fewer Aborigines around who are fluent in the old languages. In many cases the younger generation do not speak the language of their fathers, so they are immediately cut off from any real contact with their tribal mythology. Thus, any religious responses that might be derived from the possibilities extant in language are lost.

This is precisely the situation that Aborigines find them- selves in today. How often have I heard the Elders attribute the decline of their culture to the decline of their language base. Bill Neidjie, a Kakadu tribesman, poignantly expressed the dilemma when he said:

> My people all dead.
> We only got few left . . . that's all
> not many.
> We getting too old.
> Young people . . .
> I don't know if they can hold on to this story.
> But now you know this story, and you'll be coming
>     to earth.

You'll be part of the earth when you die.
You responsible now.
You got to go with this earth.
Might be you can hang on . . .
hang onto this story . . . to this earth.[4]

Or when David Mowaljarlai said: 'But when the old men die, all this knowledge will be dead-gone. The stories we told these missionaries and anthropologists are all locked up, maybe thrown out at times. The next generation will never know how to put the culture together again.'[5]

The point both these men make is that their myth life, and therefore their culture, is intimately linked to language. Clearly there are many things that cannot be put into words, which means they can only be explored through other forms of expression. In other words, they can only 'make themselves manifest'.[6] It is at this moment that myth and legend come into their own. They are perfect vehicles for the exploration of non-material realities that defy the logic of language and rational thought. Myth is a reliable tool *par excellence* of knowing designed to extract from disparate material in nature a workable hypothesis for understanding the world.

No better explanation for the way in which myth works can be found than in exploring the following story belonging to the Adnyamathanha people of the Flinders Ranges in South Australia. Their story, pertaining to death and dissolution, bodily resurrection and spiritual ascension, is a complex response to observations they have derived from nature. Using the vehicle of a conversation between Adambara, the spider, and Artapudapuda, a small crawling insect (also known as 'rotten grass tree' because of its appearance) which lives under the bark of the River Red Gum and is said to attack spiders, they are able to embrace opposing ideas in a uniquely satisfying way.

Adambara and Artapudapuda sat together and had a talk. They were sorting out what should happen when people became so sick that they died. They went away to think about it for a while, then they came back together again to make a decision.

Artapudapuda said when a Yura [black man] died, his body should stay in the grave and rot, and only his spirit should rise after three days.

Adambara said no, that is not what he wanted. When a Yura died, he said, he should be wrapped up in a web with a trap door, and the door closed and left for three days. During this time, there would be a healing process and, at the end of the three days, he would come out, just as a butterfly comes out of a cocoon. This is what Adambara wanted for humans.

Artapudapuda, however, won the argument, and the two insects went their separate ways. After a while Artapudapuda realized that his relations were dying, and he wasn't seeing them again. He was getting really upset about it. He was

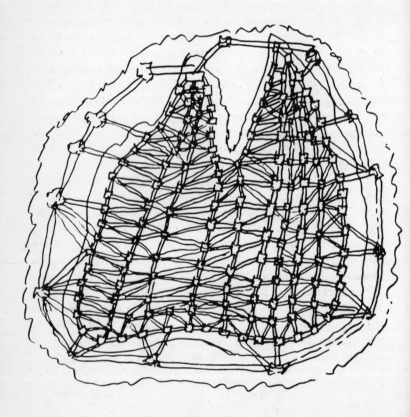

Fig. 8 Map of mythic Australia, according to David Mowaljarlai. The square nodes represent stories; the lines linking each story are lines of communication between tribes. Thus Australia is not a 'landmass' but a 'story mass'.

ashamed of the decision which he had made, and hid himself
under the bark of a wida [River Red Gum] tree.

Adambara, on the other hand, knew he had tried his best for
Yuras and was not ashamed. He stayed out in the open. This
is why even today Artapudapuda is always hiding under the
bark of a wida tree, whereas Adambara is always out where
he can be seen.[7]

Here we find a highly individual metaphysical response by
Aborigines to observable phenomena. It is clear that this myth
forces them to confront the problem of death, resurrection and
spiritual ascension, as well as the normal yearning to retain
bodily form after death, in much the same manner as more
established religious doctrines have done. Resurrection on the
third day is a common motif (compare with the Nicene Creed,
which says, 'The third day He rose again from the dead; He
ascended into heaven') among many disciplines as a method
of prolonging spiritual afterlife, without the burden of the
physical body. At the same time, the myth juxtaposes two
creatures from nature in a way that highlights the dilemma,
so that it might be accepted intellectually as well as spiritually. As Annie Coulhard (an Adnyamathanha tribeswoman)
remarked, 'Whenever a Yura died our mother used to tell us
how Adambara said to Artapudapuda, "Let him rise from the
dead." But Artapudapuda had replied, "No, let him lie there
until he rots."'[8] Such an explanation makes it relatively easy
for a child to absorb metaphysical information, and accept
into the very fibre of his being if not bodily resurrection, then
at least spiritual ascension as a viable alternative.

The success of this myth, however, lies in the way two insects
are made the carriers of a metaphysical belief. Adambara, the
spider, who lives in the open and is therefore non-secretive
and 'light' in his view of spiritual transformation, is the vehicle
for one aspect of Earth wisdom. Artapudapuda, on the other
hand, because of his secretive nature, and his inclination
to hide under bark, represents a 'darker', more material
world-view, and ultimately a lonelier perspective when it
comes to desiring literal bodily transformation after death.
Furthermore, Adambara's desire that all dead men should be
wrapped in a web with a trap door for three days prefigures
burial customs which are adhered to even today. Most tribes

accept that the spirit ultimately quits the deceased three days after death. They are always on the lookout for a sign by which the spirit has commenced its celestial journey to Vukarnaawi, across the Sea of the Dead. This is usually given in the form of a small hole at the head end of a grave (see Chapter 8).

More significantly, perhaps, the myth reinforces Aborigines' reliance on observation to enhance their metaphysical speculations. By dispensing with the strictures of logic and rationalization, they are able to explore issues these more formal techniques are unable to isolate. The idea of the spirit undergoing a period of healing, from which it emerges 'as a butterfly from a cocoon'[9] – that is, in a state of pristine beauty – in order to lead life in a more luminary sphere is a profound statement on the condition of the soul after death. It implies an extremely sensitive view of the afterlife which finds its parallel among other religious disciplines. That the spider weaving a web in the open should reflect such knowledge emphasizes the close relationship between nature and speculative thought for Aborigines. The crawler, too, by its concealed life under the bark, not only justifies its natural habits, but further highlights the limitation of bodily transformation after death. What one sees and observes with one's senses is enhanced with an extra metaphysical dimension as soon as one invokes the myth. We are not far away here from Swedenborg's Doctrine of Correspondences which suggested that each earthly idea had its counterpart in heaven.

Where the process of myth fulfils its most potent symbolic ordering of belief is in the area of landscape. Aborigines, as we have already seen, are deeply attached to their land. Alone among traditional peoples they have made the land into a variegated icon capable of embodying all that they believe. Landscape is mythologized so completely that there is hardly any countryside not accounted for in myth and story. The only exception to this rule is where land is regarded as 'rubbish country' by Aborigines, presumably because of its lack of djang or supernatural power. While creation stories may lack the drama we normally associate with myth, they nevertheless enable Aborigines to interpret their land so that it is meaningful. They have no desire to regard their land as inert, dead matter. As far as they are concerned the imprints of the Sky Heroes during the time of the Dreaming reflect a sense of continuity when these imprints are identified as physical realities on the landscape. The creation myth of the creek system around Lake Frome in South Australia is typical of many myths accounting for the creation of other natural formations in Australia.

A long time ago there was a big snake [the Rainbow Snake] called Akurra who lived up in the ranges. He was thirsty, so he went down to Lake Frome for a drink. He drank a lot of salt water at the lake. In fact, he drank the lake dry.

Akurra drank so much salt water that his belly became bloated and he became heavy. As he lumbered up towards his home in the ranges, his belly carved out a great gorge. He also made lots of waterholes where he camped in the gorge as he climbed back up into the hills. The first of these waterholes was Akurrula Awi.

He kept on coming up, gouging out the gorge, until he came to Nuldanuldanha. He camped here and made another big waterhole. From here he went on to Valivalinha, and made another waterhole. After that, the next important waterhole that he made was Adlyu Vundhu Awi.

From here he went on to Mainwater Pound [an Anglicized place-name]. He kept on climbing up the creek until he arrived at Yaki Awi, and there he stopped. This is where he came to stay for the rest of his life, and he is still there today.

He often comes up out of the waterhole at Yaki and makes rumbling noises. He lies there sunbaking and while the sun makes him warm, he makes loud rumbling noises in his belly. You can hear that big rumbling noise from a long way away.[10]

The story gives a graphic account of the creation of all the major waterholes between Lake Frome and Mainwater Pound. It is not an eventful myth, though it does situate important landmarks and register their creation. It even accounts for periodic fault-line movement in the earth whenever the Great Snake's stomach rumbles. But what this myth does is implant on the landscape a visual metaphor of the Great Snake, his massive, serpentine body stretching across the land in the throes of creation. Akurra's journey, however, does take on permutations, some of them profoundly sad, when he continues on his way. The following subsidiary myth reflects beliefs and experiences with an overlay of far more recent, post-European contact material:

> Akurra was camped at Akurra Vadnhi [Mt Fitton]. Here he got up and went from there down to the Talc Mine, and there he died. Akurra was lying there dead, and his fat was dripping out in liquid form. It went rotten. Now the white fellows [Europeans] are taking Akurra's fat and making big money out of it. It was the Yuras [Aborigines] who showed them that big history.[11]

This story portrays a deep sense of disillusionment and frustration with the way things are. The final comment suggests that Akurra's fat has been exploited by Europeans to the detriment of Aborigines. The talc has been mined with no recompense to the traditional owners. The 'big history' in this sense turned out to be economically valuable to one party only. Thus Akurra's world-creating journey has been tampered with, causing Aborigines to lament the loss of their secret knowledge.

Other, more dramatic myth cycles do enhance the land with a certain majesty. The myth cycles associated with Uluru (Ayers Rock) are some of the most dramatic of all. Great battles, tales of heroism and sacrifice account for many of the events that are recounted there by Pitjantjara tribesmen. Principal among these is the confrontation between the Liru or poisonous snake people and the Kunia or carpet snake people. These account for the creation of many of the features on the southern side of the outcrop, particularly Mutitjilda Gorge where Wanambi, the Rainbow Snake, resides. The following is an account of the creation of Uluru:

> Divided into two halves roughly corresponding to sunrise and sunset, the Djindalagul (sunny side) and Wumbuluru (shady side) separate Uluru into two major myth cycles whose central theme provides inspiration for both. It must be remembered, however, that at the time when these Dreaming events took place Uluru did not exist. The plain was, rather, a flat expanse dominated by Uluru waterhole and Mutitjilda Spring where Wanambi lived. The sunny and shady sides of Ayers Rock corresponded to the territories of two groups of Sky Heroes, the Mala or Hare-wallaby people (sunny side) and the Kunia or carpet snake people (shady side). At the time of the Dreaming

these two groups lived in relative harmony, content to inhabit the Djindalagul and Wumbuluru (light and shade).

In the Petermann Ranges, far to the west, lived a tribe known as the Windulka or Mulga seed people. Deciding to initiate their youths, they asked the bell bird, Panpanpalana, to fly throughout the region and invite all to attend. The invitation was received with delight by the Kunia people who agreed to travel west to the Petermanns. The Mala people, however, were in the midst of initiation ceremonies of their own and were unwilling to make the journey. Furthermore, they were reluctant to supply their much prized eagle chick, Kedrun, to the Windulka who required its down for their body paintings.

Meanwhile the Kunia people camped the first night of their trek westward at Uluru waterhole (now a deep catchment on the summit of the Rock) where they met up with a number of sleepy lizard women. Enamoured, they decided to ignore the Mulga seed men's invitation, and instead settle down with the sleepy lizard girls around Mutitjilda Spring.

Deep in the Petermanns the Mulga seed men waited for their guests. After several days, and with still no sign of their arrival,

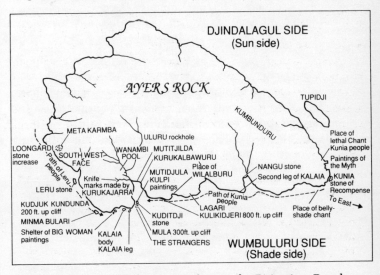

Fig. 9   Myth map of Uluru, according to the Pitjantjara People, showing major landmarks of the Mutitjilda conflict. (From Bill Harney, *Ayers Rock and Beyond*.)

they ordered Panpanpalana, the bell bird, to return to the Uluru region and ascertain what had happened. Reminding the Mala and Kunia people of their obligations to attend the Mulga seed ceremonies, bell bird was confronted with excuses. The Kunia people maintained that they had recently married, while the Mala rather rudely insisted they were busily occupied with their own initiation ceremonies.

Bell bird's message on his return to the Mulga seed men made them angry. They were affronted by this lack of courtesy from people they had always regarded as friends. Their refusal to attend the rituals in Petermann country signalled the beginning of a conflict, the repercussions of which still live on today. The Mulga seed Elders had decided that both tribes must be punished, and they set about enacting their edict in a most unusual way.

Firstly, the Mulga seed *mekigars* [medicine men] decided to create an evil-spirit dingo, Kulpunya. The clever-men built a skeletal frame out of mulga branches, forked sticks and women's hair on the ground. At one end they placed wallaby teeth, at the other end the tail of a bandicoot. For the rest of the day the clever-men chanted songs designed to invoke the spirit of evil. At sunset they left Kulpunya, the devil-dog, alone, knowing that in darkness its being would be fully realized. By morning Kulpunya had grown large teeth and its feet had formed. Hairless, Kulpunya was more vicious in its behaviour than any crocodile. The devil-dog was now ready to attack the Mala people and destroy them.

Kulpunya arrived at Uluru while everyone was having their afternoon nap. Only Lorin, the old Kingfisher woman, remained awake. Her cries of warning were stifled by the devil-dog who proceeded to kill her. Then it attacked the rest of the Mala people, killing many. Those who managed to survive fled in confusion towards the southwest, never to return. They had been driven from Uluru by Kulpunya at the behest of the Mulga seed men and their lives, which had been surrounded by light and ritual, were now destroyed. Their world, graced as it was by the eagle chick, Kedrun, symbol of all that was perfect in ritual initiation, had been turned into a mausoleum.

But the Mulga seed men reserved the greatest retribution for the Kunia. Calling upon their friends, the Liru or poisonous snake people, a band of Sky Heroes who lived at Katatjuta (the Olgas), they asked them to attack the Kunia on their behalf and destroy them. Under their leader, Kulikitjeri, the Liru approached Uluru from the southwest, there to confront the Kunia people, lead by the young warrior Ungata. A mighty battle ensued near Mutitjilda Spring. Spears were thrown. At the height of the battle Bulari Minma [minma = married woman] gave birth to a child in a cave not far from the scene of battle. While she lay there in labour Kulikitjeri and Ungata were exchanging blows. Though severely wounded in the head, Kulikitjeri still managed to inflict a mortal wound to Ungata's leg, causing him to bleed profusely. The young Kunia warrior retreated into Mutitjilda gorge where he lay down to die.

Demoralized by the loss of their leader, the Kunia people began to retreat to the east. It was not until then that Ingridi, Ungata's mother, hearing that her son was dying, decided to avenge him. She quickly gathered up her digging stick and spat a mystical substance known as *arukwita* on it. Then she entered the fray, first seeking out Kulikitjeri in the hope of killing him. Empowered by *arukwita*, Ingridi's digging stick made her invincible. Kulikitjeri was unable to shield himself from her blows and soon lost his nose in the fight. His death in battle gave new hope to the Kunia people who quickly rallied and counterattacked. One of the Liru men, however, when he saw that they were likely to be driven off, and out of sheer frustration at the death of his leader, decided to attack the sleepy lizard women in their camp. It was, after all, the sleepy lizard women who had caused the fracas in the first place. He put their camp to the torch.

Burning down the sleepy lizards' camp signalled an end to the battle. The Kunia picked up their dying leader and retreated to the east. Ungata's death, soon after, caused such an outpouring of grief among his people that all of them gathered around him and sung themselves to death. Their mass suicide, together with the invasion by the Liru and the devil-dog's attack on the Mala elsewhere, caused such tremendous ructions within the earth itself that finally Uluru rose from the ashes of the sleepy lizards' camp to grace the land as a monument. Though the spirit of the Mala and Kunia people may have been broken by these attacks orchestrated by the the Mulga seed men from the Petermanns, Uluru embraced their every action and made them a part of itself.[12]

It is clear that the sunny side of Uluru reflected an Eden at the time of the Dreaming. The Mala people lived in a land of plenty, performing their ceremonies without concern for the world beyond. They ignored the entreaties of those who lived to the west 'towards the sunset', and who required of them help in matters of ritual. They were content to exist for themselves only, impervious to the needs of those less fortunate than themselves. As a result, evil was sent among them in the form of the devil-dog, Kulpunya. Dissension and strife were sent to arouse them from their apathy. Their disdain for the Mulga seed men resulted in their exile from Djindalagul, the 'sunny side' of Uluru, the land of primordial delight. They had been condemned to live a life of wandering, far from their homeland.

No other landscape in Australia records such an epic encounter between the spirits. On the shady side, the Sky Heroes of the Dreaming had acted out a battle reminiscent of the Trojan war or the confrontation between Arjuna and Karna in the *Bhagavad-Gita*. Kulikitjeri against Ungata, Achilles against Hector – these pairs of opposites confront one another across aeons. The sleepy lizard women find an echo in Helen who provoked war between Greece and Troy. Hecuba's lament at the death of her son Hector varies little from that of Ingridi's. Whether it is on the fields of Troy or in the pages of the *Mahabharata*, the outcome is always one of tragedy and triumph. Epic lays pronounce victory over death, feats of courage, and the final apotheosis of peoples. For the Kunia, ever slavish to their passions, the Battle of Mutitjilda was one where they were defeated by the warlike Liru, themselves no more than loyal emissaries of a people who stood for the inviolability of ceremony and ritual.

This myth cycle is embalmed in stone at Uluru. Mutitjilda Gorge records the battle between the Liru and the Kunia as various topographic features. Three rock holes, high on Uluru itself, are where Ungata bled to death. The rainwater that fills them today and flows down Uluru's slopes into Wanambi's pool is regarded as the transubstantiated blood of the dying Ungata. High on the cliff face itself a number of dark stains represent the red ochre mourning marks Ingridi daubed on her body after she had vanquished Kulikitjeri. Lower down, the white stains made by the mystic substance known as arukwita can be seen. Kulikitjeri's severed nose lies on the ground at the head of the gorge. On the eastern rock face three vertical gashes record the wounds inflicted by Ungata on Kulikitjeri. A large cave nearby is the womb of the married woman, Bulmari Minma, who gave birth to a child. The child lies on the ground at the entrance as a large stone.

## MYTH AND THE LANDSCAPE

Uluru is a complex network of mythic motifs which interlace as topographic features. For most Aborigines throughout Australia, Uluru is the true navel of the earth. More importantly, the continent is seen as a gigantic human body which all Aborigines are familiar with because of a unique story sharing system known as *wunnan*.[13] According to Mowarljarlai, in the pre-European contact days Aborigines used to share their knowledge along the numerous trade routes that criss-crossed the country.

> The whole of Australia is *Bandaiyan*. The front we call *wadi*, the belly section, because the continent is lying down flat on its back. It is just sticking out from the surface of the ocean. Deep down underneath are the buttocks, *wambalma* – from where the leg joints run into the pelvis and right across to the other side.
>
> Inside the body is *Wunggud [ungud]*, the Snake. She grows all of nature on the outside of her body. The sides are *unggnu djullu*, rib section. This rib section goes right across the country, above the navel. *Uluru* is the navel, the centre – *wangigit*.
>
> The part below the navel is *wambut*, the pubic section. There is a woman's section – *njambut*, and a man's section – *ambut*.
>
> Right up top is the head part, *ulangun* – Cape York, Arnhem Land, Kimberley, Bathurst and Melville Island . . . Below the Gulf of Carpentaria are the lungs, *wumangnalla*.[14]

The attribution of human form to the earth in this way is often regarded as indicative of an early stage of intellectual development. It is said that preliterate peoples are at pains to identify with their land as if it were a physiological or psychological 'echo' of themselves. Yet Mowarljarlai's testament is reminiscent of a nineteenth-century German mystic's account of a similar perception when he saw the earth as an 'Angel':

> I was walking in the open air on a beautiful spring morning. The wheat was growing green, the birds were singing, the dew was sparkling, the smoke rising; a transfiguring light lay over everything; this was only a tiny fragment of Earth ... and yet the idea seemed to me not only beautiful, but also so true and obvious that she was an Angel – an Angel so sumptuous, so fresh, so like a flower and at the same time so firm and so composed, who was moving through the sky ... that I asked myself how it was possible that men should have blinded themselves to the point of seeing Earth as nothing but a dried-up mass.[15]

Clearly the art of myth imposes its own criteria upon how the world should be seen. That landscape is the 'bones' of Aboriginal myth making suggests a new (in reality, an old) way of looking at the earth. It implies a metaphysical structure within the earth that enables it to transcend its material limitations, and so enter the minds of men as a symbolic image. This metaphysical structure Feschner saw in the earth as an 'Angel'. Aborigines, on the other hand, see it as djang – that quality of Earth wisdom which partakes of the divine. The Aborigines teach us that to ignore its power is to ignore its capacity to transform the individual. Equally, to regard the earth as no more than a passive material condition is to fall into the trap of exploiting it for its own sake. Rearranging our environment, after all, has become the hallmark of our modern age.

For Aborigines their myths embody supreme realities. When these are lost, then their culture will die. Language, myth and landscape are intimately linked in an endless knot of metaphysical possibilities. By taking any one element away from them (that is, by refusing Aborigines the right of land ownership, or insisting that they learn English to the detriment of their own language) it is possible to destroy their reality so completely that they begin to destroy themselves. In some areas of Queensland, for example, where the State Government has refused the tribes genuine land tenure, the suicide rate has risen to become the highest in the world. Alcoholism, disease and disillusionment are all symptoms of Aboriginal self-destruction brought on by prolonged, and in some cases irreversible separation from their myth life. With no access to their land, there is no access to myth by way of ritual or ceremony.

The language of myth is at pains to separate ordinary reality from that of the events of the Dreaming. In doing so, it allows Aborigines to range free over a realm of the imagination which belongs to the Soul of the universe. For it is clear that the Dreaming represents just that: a supreme interworld of archetypal images which themselves partake of revelation. The contact between Aborigines and the Sky Heroes of the Alcheringa is made permanent by myth, while the process is completed in the act of drawing landscape into the equation. Landscape alone holds the key to understanding the un-revealed nature of the Dreaming. This is because landscape is the true language of myth. Words are only adjuncts, as are chants and ceremonies. Therefore in order to understand, indeed revere the earth, Aborigines maintain that we must learn to interpret landscape in a way that reveals to us its inherent power, its Angel, its djang. It is the one lesson that we must all set ourselves to learn before it is too late.

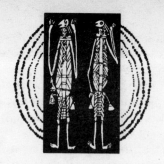

# 6 · CLEVER MEN AND THEIR DREAMS

In all traditions there must be one person in whom the primary spiritual aspirations of a people are centred. It is not possible for a culture to survive for very long without the charismatic presence of someone who acts as a custodian of magical lore to which the rest of the tribe adheres as a matter of course. Among the great religions the priest, mufti, monk or brahman occupies such a position. Around such people a certain aura prevails – an aura born of sanctity and community respect. These men are responsible for the rites; they are healer of men's souls; they are often called upon to perform miraculous cures. As a result they are usually revered and sometimes even feared. Ambivalently placed, they inhabit two worlds – those of the spirit and of men. Yet they fulfil the role of drawing these two worlds together for the sake of both. Celestial harmony is as much their concern as the well-being of individual souls.

Among Aborigines, such a position is filled by the *karadji* or *mekigar*. Each tribe has a different name for him, though his actual role is always the same. Among the Wuradjeri, he was known as *wiri:nan*, meaning 'powerful man' or *bug:nja* ('spirit', or 'spirit of the whirlwind') as it was the custom of his spirit-self to travel in a whirlwind. He was also regarded as *walemira*, which means not only clever in the normal sense, but also intellectually clever. Sometimes he was called walemira *talmai* which means 'one to whom cleverness has been handed on'.[1] In nearly all instances it was acknowledged that his 'power' (*miwi*) was derived from his predecessors, and by implication from the Alcheringa itself.

To the nineteenth-century settlers, in contrast, he was looked upon as a scamp or charlatan, a man who used trickery and sometimes fear in order to preserve his tribal status. Yet it was he who they first endeavoured to discredit whenever they wished to subjugate a tribe. Missionaries were also quick to isolate him so that they might assume the responsibility of guiding Aboriginal souls to Christ. In the early years of European contact the karadji found himself a prime target for ridicule. If his 'medicine' could be shown to be ineffectual, then his hold upon a tribe might be loosened. By sowing the seeds of doubt and suspicion about his powers, in time his extinction was assured. As one informant remarked, regretting the passing of the clever-men from his community, 'We don't have any old men like that any more. They all gone. We don't know their secrets.' The secrets he was referring to were those of medicinal and metaphysical knowledge.

## TRAINING OF NOVICES

Becoming a karadji varied across Australia, but the principal requirements were the same. A man who wished to become a clever-man was either 'called' by the *Iruntarinia* or *Oruncha* spirits, or he was initiated into the craft by another karadji. In the former cases, a man subjected himself to initiation at the hands of spirit-beings from the Dreaming, usually at their behest. As an ancestral reincarnation, the Iruntarinia was capable of transporting a man 'out of himself' for the duration of the initiation in order that he might become 'reborn' as a karadji. Generally speaking, a postulant was regarded as someone different, unlike his fellow tribesmen in behaviour or demeanour. He was a man prepared to undergo an initiation which involved some pain so that he might be called a karadji.

Among the Central Desert tribes, when a man felt that he was capable of becoming a karadji, he usually walked away from camp alone until he came to the mouth of a cave. Here he lay down to sleep, or fell into a trance, while remaining careful not to venture inside the cave itself. To do so would have been to acquire the power too quickly and be spirited away forever. At dawn he was visited by an Iruntarinia who proceeded to spear him in the neck. The spear was then said to pass through the man's tongue, leaving a hole large enough to admit a finger. This scar remained with the man for the rest of his life. A second lance was thrown by the Iruntarinia which pierced the man's head from ear to ear, resulting in his 'death'. The victim was finally carried into the cave which opened into a land of perpetual sunshine and running water. Here he was subjected to a major operation in which his bodily organs were removed and replaced with new ones. When he came back to life and 'awoke' from his trance, the man was no longer himself. To emphasize his changed condition the man experienced a period of insanity. It was after he had fully recovered that the Iruntarinia deigned to lead him back to his people. Other karadji and dogs are said to be the only ones able to see the Iruntarinia standing beside the man. To the rest of the tribe the spirit was invisible.[2]

The presence of the Iruntarinia is further reflected in the initiation of Clever-men among the Wuradjeri people in the east. After acquiring special instruction from a practising karadji, a postulant receives a secondary totem (bala) which is 'sung' into him. This totem can only be released by recitation of the necessary songs while undergoing a period of ritual concentration, or meditation. Several years after this event the postulant receives word from his father, or his father's father, that the great Baiame has intimated to them that he is willing to meet with him. At a particular gathering, where other clever-men are present, Baiame appears. He is distinguished from other people by the 'light radiating from his eyes'. From his mouth he produces sacred water called gali, said to be liquified quartz crystal. This is said to fall on the postulant and enter him, causing feathers to appear some time after. As Baiame departs these feathers turn into wings in preparation for his first flight in the company of the All-father. Later, Baiame 'sings' a piece of quartz crystal into his head so that he will have X-ray vision. Baiame also removes a sacred fire (wi:meju) from his own body and 'sings' it into the postulant's chest. His wings are then removed, and he is allowed to return to his guardians. The final rite involves the 'singing' into a postulant of a thick sinew cord (maulwe, or aerial rope) which is later used in magical practices. The man is now a fully fledged clever-man or doctor.[3]

According to tradition, Baiame came from Kating-ngara ('from the other side of the sea') to the west. In him rested all power, whether religious or magical. Before the advent of Europeans he 'was always amongst the people long ago'. Their arrival caused Baiame to retreat to his homeland, Kating-ngara, through fear. After that, he returned only intermittently to attend the initiation of clever-men. Thus the power of these men ultimately derived from that of Baiame. He alone 'made' a karadji, exhorting him not to quarrel or fight with other clever-men. To do so would only diminish the prestige of all clever-men. In this way, the karadji became exemplars of Baiame here on earth.[4]

Another variation of this ceremony involves the postulant's descent down a tunnel to a strange country, Kating-ngara, 'on the other side of the sea'. On his arrival Baiame grabbed him about the waist, placed him on top of his head and walked away with him to his cave. There he set him down and gazed at him with X-ray eyes. Looking into his mind, he asked, 'Have you been made into a man?' To which the postulant replied, 'Yes'. Baiame then asked, 'Have you been prepared by your father in order that you might receive my power and my knowledge?' The man answered, 'Yes'. Baiame responded, 'All right. I will fix you up.'

During the three days of their encounter, in which the postulant was 'made a man again', Baiame 'sang' the quartz crystal into him and instilled the sacred flame in his breast. Baiame also poured the sacred gali water over the man and the man acquired feathers. When he had learnt all that there was to know from Baiame, the Spirit informed him that he was now ready to return to his people.

Among the Dieri on the edge of Sturt Stony Desert in Central Australia, a postulant is taken out into the bush by a gungi, or clever-man, who is ritually decorated, where he undergoes a period of seclusion and meditation. On leaving camp he is mourned by his parents as if he were now dead to them. He then enters a state of trance during which the spirit visits him and replaces his human mind with a 'gungi mind'. Powerful gifts are then bestowed upon him which can be used in performing magic. Reborn as a karadji, he now possesses a spirit snake in his stomach and is capable of flying into the sky-world by means of a hair cord where he is able to drink water which gives him power.

On the other hand, a man who is initiated by a fellow clever-man is more severely tested. He is taken to a secluded spot, made to stand with his hands behind his head, and told that whatever happens he must remain completely silent. The karadji then withdraws from his own body a number of small crystals which are placed one by one in the hollow of a spear-thrower. The postulant is then grasped from behind by others. The crystals are pressed into his body, beginning at the legs and later moving up to his chest. Of course some blood flows from the wounds. Crystals are then projected into the man's head from a distance. These same crystals are also forced up under the nail of one of his fingers. Such a process is carried out over a period of three days. His tongue also receives an incision. Finally, his body is rubbed all over with grease and an Oruncha design is drawn on his forehead and chest. A crown of leaves and fur are placed on his head. He is ordered to remain silent until his tongue wound has healed. He must abstain from eating fat of any kind, and must not touch the flesh of dogs, fish or echidna. He may eat the marrow of bones, but only if the bones are broken.

Though the ritual of initiation into the order of karadji varies across Australia, the essentials remain the same. Quartz crystals, as a symbol of the All-father's power, are present in most cases and form the basis for ritual baptism. The acquisition of the 'sacred fire' of the All-father and the permanent link with Him by way of the aerial rope ensures that the postulant knows from where his power comes. So too does the trance condition and that sense of departing from oneself. The whole object of the initiation process is to 'bury' the old man and replace it with the new man. Symbolic removal of the internal organs emphasizes this transformation. The use of feathers is a popular convention for expressing spiritual transformation as Plato himself mentions: 'A man beholds the beauty of the world, is reminded of truth and beauty, and his wings begin to grow.' (*Phaedrus* 249e).[5] Whatever the postulant may learn from his teachers in the way of technique must be seen in terms of the need to preserve a distance between a karadji and other members of the tribe. Certain psychic powers need to be centred on the individual, otherwise he will not have the presence to heal illness, resolve spiritual or psychic disorders, enact curses and, in general, act as a tribal hierophant. The solemn air about his demeanour strengthens his authority so that he may carry out his profession with purpose.

## SPECIAL QUALITIES

According to one informant, you could always recognize a clever-man 'by the intelligent look in his eyes.'[6] Berndt remarked that the great ones were 'enveloped in peculiar atmosphere which caused people to feel different'. The karadji's psychic power and knowledge of esoteric magic and sacred lore set him apart from his contemporaries. Elkin recalled a clever-man that he met from whose 'immobile face, shine shrewd, penetrating eyes – eyes that look you all the way through'. This man was an 'outstanding person, a clear thinker, a man of decision, one who believed, and acted on belief', who possessed the power to 'will others to have faith in themselves'.[7] Clearly these men were endowed with a unique, forceful character which enabled them to act as tribal hierophants and doctors. Self-discipline, preceded by training, enabled such men to make contact with powerful spiritual and psychological forces in order to benefit the tribe as a whole.

Another central concept in the making of a karadji is that of mummification. The symbolic removal of the abdominal organs from the postulant by either the Oruncha spirits or his associates suggests a desire to preserve the aspirant as a 'raised' human being. His new organs extend to him a 'new' life in keeping with his changed status. In other words, a karadji becomes a new man, someone different, a person whose sole purpose from hereon is to serve his community, using magical techniques which are the traditional preserve of his profession. His changed condition is further emphasized by his encounter with Baiame 'in the sky', or the belief that his power is bestowed upon him by the Rainbow Snake. Quartz crystals and spirit-snakes provide a sacramental link with the otherworld. One informant who had in some dream or vision 'imagined himself to have been taken by his father on a thread (i.e. cord) to the "Camp of Baiame", beyond the sky,' met Daramulum, (the Supreme Being, a pseudonym for Baiame) who was 'a very aged man seated in a kneeling position, with a quartz crystal extending from each shoulder to the sky above – that is to say, a second sky from the earth'.[8]

His mystic power, too, depended on the observance of certain food taboos. For example, among the Central Australian tribes, a karadji must refrain from eating the flesh of a kangaroo which is known to have been feeding on new green grass.[9] He should not eat fat or warm meat, nor inhale smoke from burning bones.[10] Such food taboos served as a constant reminder to the karadji of his status within the tribe. He must be seen to act differently from other members of his tribe if he is to be respected as a hierophant.

The karadji's psychic power is also legendary. Elkin believes that their telepathic and clairvoyant abilities stem from the silence and solitude of the Australian bush, conditions he regarded as favourable to meditation and receptivity. In any event, there are stories recorded of how such men are able to 'talk' with distant strangers using telepathic powers. One such case was recorded among the Lower Murray River people by R. M. Berndt in a letter to Elkin:

> When a man is down on the plain and I am on the hill, I look towards him while I am talking. He sees me and turns towards me. I say, 'Do I hear?' I move my head from side to side glaring at him, and at last stare at him. And then, turning, I say, 'Come on quickly'. As I stare at him fixedly, I see him turn as he feels my stare. He then turns and looks about while I continue staring at him. So I say, 'Walk this way, right along here, where I am sitting.' Then he walks right up to me where I am sitting behind a bush. I draw him with my power (*miwi*).

You do not see any hand signs or hear any shouting. At last he comes up and nearly falls over me. I call out so that he will see me. He says, 'You talked to me and I *felt* [author's italics] it. How did you talk so?' I explain, and he adds: 'I felt your words while you were talking to me, and then I feel that you are there.' I answer: 'True, it was in that way that I talked to you, and you felt those words and also that power'.[11]

Paranormal activity further enhances a karadji's standing within the tribe. He is accredited with the ability to travel astrally, often covering vast distances in a day. It is said that they are able to run less than a metre above the ground, carried along in an envelope of 'solidified air' Whether in a trance or under self-hypnosis, it is clear that a clever-man is able to attain to a kind of anaesthesia which deadens the senses so that he does not feel the weight of his own body. In this way he is able to enjoy a 'light, agreeable dizziness' which enables him to walk at an unaccustomed speed.

An example of this type of travel was related to Elkin in the following manner:

A doctor was with some other Aborigines at the horse-yard on a station where they were working. When the rest set out for camp, about 400 metres away, he remained at the yard, saying that he would catch up to them. When, however, they reached their camp, he [i.e. the doctor] was sitting there making a boomerang, as though he had not been away. They did not see him pass, and there were no hidden tracks by which he could have hurried around.[12]

His materialization at the camp, or indeed at the yard, appears to have been deliberately provoked by the clever-man as a method of enhancing his status among his peers. Nevertheless, such displays of astral travel were merely an external manifestation of the inward spiritual power these men were acknowledged to possess. For every trickster wishing to demonstrate his prowess there were other men who preferred to engage in meditation and contemplation of a high order as a sign of their calling.

This is not to say that clever-men did not congregate to exchange magical ideas on occasions. At a sacred playground, known as gu:te'kiri, they would arrive along a pathway from the west, leaving the main body of the tribe at the corroboree ground. Here a bullroarer, the voice of Baiame, would be sounded prior to a period of singing. The singing induced a meditative or trance-like state conducive to magical performance. Lying on their backs under a tree, the clever-men would 'sing out' their buru:maulwe, or testes cord, which in turn evolved into their respective maulwe, the aerial rope mentioned earlier. In the manner of a spider secreting gossamer they would then begin climbing up the cord, hand over hand, until they reached the top of the tree. When the bullroarer sounded again these men would descend the tree.

Another magical demonstration of the aerial rope was conducted in association with fire. Berndt was told about a meeting of clever-men near Ivanhoe (NSW) by Jack King, held in 1882, at his own initiation into the brotherhood. He spoke of how Joe Dagan, another clever-man, announced to all that evening that 'he was going to show them tonight what they never seen perhaps'.

> We all got to the sacred ground, and the old men made a big fire – a very big fire. Dagan then said: 'You fellows sit down around that fire and watch it.'
>
> The big mob of men all sat round the fire staring into it. Then Dagan went out a bit from the fire where there was a clear space, and lay down full length at the top of a slight rise which sloped down towards the fire. He began to roll slowly down towards the fire; he passed through the people who had made a space for him, and rolled into the blazing fire. Once in it, he rolled about making the sound 'fi: 'fi: 'fi: and scattered the coals in every direction. All the people were staring at him in the fire. After a while he got up and walked out of the fire and stood alongside the others. The European clothes he wore were unharmed, 'just as if he had never been in the fire'. There was no doubting that he had gone through the fire, because all those men present had seen him in it with their own eyes.
>
> Dagan then went over to the butt of a big tree standing nearby, and proceeded to crawl up the tree in a special manner. With all the men watching him, he lay down on his body, his legs wide apart and suspended above the ground. He then sung to himself (so that no one could hear his words), and his maulwe cord

gradually came out of his testes, and went directly upwards. He climbed up this and reached the top of the tree where there was a nest about forty feet from the ground. While climbling he was in exactly the same position – head well back, body outstretched, legs apart, and arms to the side – as when he 'sang out' his cord.[13]

It is evident from the description of these events that we are witnessing certain paranormal practices relating to spiritual ascent and renewal. Climbing a rope or a tree into the sky is common to many beliefs. Homer in the *Iliad* (VIII, 17–27) explains how Zeus suspends a golden rope from heaven and taunts all the gods and goddesses to try and drag him from the sky. 'You will never drag Zeus, the supreme master, from the sky to the ground, however hard you try. But if I cared to pull hard from the end, I should haul you up, earth and all.' Plato uses a similar image to explain the structure of the universe when he speaks of 'a light that stretches from above across the sky and the earth, a light as straight as a pillar and very like a rainbow, but brighter and purer' (*Republic* X, 616c).

Zeus' 'golden chain' is used by the Pseudo Dionysius the Areopagite (*The Divine Names* 3,1) as a symbol for prayer:

> Let us strive therefore by our prayers to raise ourselves to the height of these divine and beneficent rays. It is as if we were to seize an infinitely bright chain hanging from the summit of the sky and descending to us, constantly striving to pull it down to us with each hand in turn. We should have the impression that we are bringing it down, but in reality our efforts would be unable to move it, for it would be present as an entirety from top to bottom, and it is we who would be raising ourselves, to the highest splendours of a bright and shining perfection.

It is significant that in India the Sun is seen as the Cosmic Weaver, and is often compared with a spider. In the *Shatapatha Brahmana* we find it repeated many times that 'the Sun binds these worlds together by a thread'. In the *Mundoko Upanishad* a similar comparison is made: 'Just as a spider draws out and draws back, so all is born in this world from the imperishable.' Furthermore, God is seen in the *Bhagavad-Gita* as the One who 'weaves' the world. Cosmological Creation, as well as the cosmos itself, are symbolized by the act of weaving.

Since dispersion and disconnectedness are equivalent to non-being, integration into the One must be given its due. The most satisfactory image to express this view is the thread, the spider, the weft and weaving. The spider's web shows the possibility of unifying space from a divine centre.[14]

The aerial rope ascending to heaven is another important motif for describing cosmic renewal. 'Do you know Kapra, the thread by which this world and the other world and all beings are bound together? He who knows the thread, the ruler within, he knows *brahman* ... he knows all things' (*Brihadaranyaka Upanishad*). A Tibetan tradition describes how Buddha came down from heaven by a staircase to 'clear a path for humankind'. The first king of Tibet was said to have come down from heaven on a rope, and to have returned up it prior to the rope being cut. The aerial rope to heaven (or into a tree) was thus a reflection of man's celestial origin before some catastrophic event changed the structure of the cosmos. Today only magicians and clever-men are able to climb heavenward with the aid of a cord.

The intermingling of the spider motif and that of the aerial rope among Aboriginal clever-men, as a reflection of celestial encounter, suggests that these people were well aware of their metaphysical implications. By the later nineteenth century it is more than likely that many of the more esoteric elements associated with such rites had been lost, however. Nevertheless, if Jack King's testimony is to be believed, the clever-men of his day were still capable of extraordinary feats of magic. Rolling in a fire before ascending on an aerial rope suggests the clever-man concerned was well aware that his ability to perform paranormal tricks, similar to those of the fakirs of India, was a prelude to the revelation of mystical knowledge to his audience. What Joe Dagan wanted to show his contemporaries was how his ability to rise above recognized sensory experience indicated the special spiritual condition that he had attained, which, in turn, was open to them as well. He was, in effect, intimating man's primordial link with Baiame, the All-father, the One who had given him the power of astral travel in the first place.

Healing the sick, performing exorcisms, determining who might be the cause of a sudden death within the tribe, pointing the bone to enact a ritual killing – these were all part of a clever-man's social responsibilities. Curative magic went hand in hand with the promotion of rain or success in hunting. It appears that a karadji was invested with singular powers of transformation. In modern parlance this means he had mastered certain psychological techniques (hypnosis, group trance, and such like) which might be used to control the minds of his people. Such a view, however, presupposes that his role was merely to trick his people, and so subjugate them, with the aid of magic. Our own researches suggest the contrary. The clever-man's essential role was one of spiritual healing, the easing of tribal tensions caused by perennial isolation, and affirming the reality of the otherworld, the Dreaming, and its metaphysical importance to man's survival. His task was to periodically 'fly' to Kating-ngara, the land of Baiame, in order to re-establish cosmic links with the All-father.

The act of mediation between the realm of the spirit and that of everyday physical reality is extremely important to the Aborigine. Totemic identity and mythic association provide him with a continuous link with the Dreaming, of course. But these more often than not merely reinforce cultural acceptance and well-being. Since they are part of what he is, there is often no need to question their relevance in the scheme of things. The clever-man's presence within a community, moreover, acts as a constant reminder of the 'power' (miwi) that pervades all things. He alone inaugurates a feeling of mystical otherness among those who look to him for guidance. In oral cultures much emphasis is place upon the possession of esoteric lore by certain members of the community. These men acquire status because of their knowledge – a knowledge that can only be shared when one of them chooses to pass it on to newly initiated postulants. Thus the chain of knowledge is forged between one generation and another without any break in the tradition. This unity between the past and the present further enhances a sense of continuity which provides Aborigines with their sense of belonging. Knowing that the karadji 'knows' certain things, and that he has insight into the magical predicament, makes it possible for others to explore whatever cultural or social reality they so wish. They are free to be hunters, dancers, songsters and weapon makers, secure in the knowledge that their contact with the spirit-world is in the hands of an expert.

In the twentieth century the relationship between the karadji and the tribe unfortunately has been ruptured. There are few clever-men left, and as a result their knowledge is largely lost. Modern medicine and government aids have assumed the responsibilities that these men once regarded as their own. Nevertheless, their disappearance from the cultural scene has left its scars. Among many tribes a disturbing cultural vacuity prevails. The people, while they may still remember many of their stories, songs and myths, and are able to perform their dances and participate in mortuary rituals, now find themselves at odds with many of the deeper levels of their culture. None of the younger men desire to learn the things their fathers knew, because they believe these things are all in the past. Those few karadji who are still alive find their status dwindling as they face an uncertain future as tribal hierophants. The sun is slowly setting on their world, a world of mystery and knowledge which once formed the metaphysical bedrock of this ancient culture.

The clever-man was the prototype for the spiritual man, the monk, who we like to regard as living jewels in more recent cultures. His special knowledge of the spirit-world equipped him to interpret metaphysical reality in a way not open to other members of the tribe. While, on the surface, his 'bag of tricks' may appear to be little more than the product of a certain amount of psychological skulduggery, such an observation dismisses the very real effect his magical paraphernalia had upon the recipient. It is more important to view his role as doctor in the light of the healing effect he engendered. His most significant role within a community was invariably his ability to transcend sensory reality, and thus intimate to others the profound importance of the Dreaming as a spiritual event. No man was so inherently associated with the fruits of meditation than the karadji. He alone was able to hold converse with Sky Heroes and translate their timeless message, so that men might draw benefit from their celestial knowledge and live out their lives in its beneficial shade.

Elkin expressed with some eloquence the relationship between a clever-man and the world when he said:

This world is believed to be the source of life in man and nature, and all initiated men are links with it. But only men of *high degree* [author's italics], men who in their special initiation have been admitted to this world in the sky and on earth – only these men can exercise that power to prevent death, to restore life, to recapture the soul, to converse with the dead, and to understand in some real measure the workings of the human mind.[15]

Clever-men are indeed 'spiders', able to weave some coherent pattern out of the disorder of disparate reality which sometimes threatens to consume us. It remains to be seen whether the tradition of the karadji will ultimately survive and renew itself, given the pressures of the modern world. If it does not, then Aboriginal culture will find itself deprived of much of its power, consigned to history as an anthropological relic whose appeal is one of nostalgia rather than as a living reality of its own.

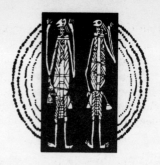

# 7 · SACRED LOVE

The idea that sexual encounters of a communal sort might echo
primordial realities is not alien to Aboriginal belief. On the
contrary, at least until the early part of this century, Aborigines
had long practised a form of group sexual activity which one
observer likened to 'sacred love'.[1] How close they were to
affirming a mode of behaviour which has disappeared from the
social context of modern man remains uncertain. The truth is,
group sexual activity has long been associated with ritual and
festival, whether they be Bacchic or Saturnalian. In the case of
Aborigines, a people who live within a network of carefully
defined tribal kin relationships, known as *mada-mala*, the
prospect for sexual encounters outside these boundaries are
strictly controlled, though not infrequent. Betrothed at an early
age according to skin affiliations, a boy or girl's sexual education is therefore largely a clandestine affair, conducted out
of sight of the elder members of the community. Nevertheless
their activities are conditioned by neither a sense of shame
nor sin.

## SEXUAL CUSTOMS

Physical attractiveness is important to young men and women.
They are at pains to appear clean and tidy, and resort to body
decorations to enhance their beauty. Washing regularly is
regarded as a sign of youth. One young Yirrkalla man, under
pressure of work and therefore unable to wash for a few days,

was concerned that if he did not wash soon he would be seen to be getting old and so prove unattractive to his wife. 'She'll be sleeping with someone else pretty soon', was his remark.

The standard of ideal beauty is often based upon certain ancestral men and women who lived at the time of the Dreaming, and who have subsequently become the inspiration for spiritual belief and ritual. An example of this type of mythic beauty is recorded by Berndt:

> The Muna Muna [i.e. daughters of the ancestral Mother, Kunapipi] were said to be of great beauty, having long copper-coloured hair, light coffee-tinted skin, firm bodies with full, rounded breasts and protuberant dark nipples, smooth rounded buttocks, an erect carriage, drawn-in abdomen and thin ankles and shins, soft brown long-lashed eyes and quivering nostrils and lips slightly apart.[2]

Here indeed was a model of beauty with which a young woman might identify.

Sexual activity among Aborigines begins at an early age. Both parties are well aware of their obligations by the time of marriage. Pre- and extra-marital relations are routinely practised, though within the confines of traditionally accepted behaviour. Sexual and emotional satisfaction, the removal of discontent or repression are carefully orchestrated so as to avoid violent unrest, quarrels or fights within the community. Uncontrolled promiscuity, which from the traditional viewpoint is illegal anyway, is frowned upon. All legalized sexual activity is confined to channels according to kinship grouping, thus preventing acts of incest between brother and sister, mother and son, father and daughter. Only under certain conditions can a 'wrong marriage' between prohibited groups be sanctioned by resorting to specific myths or stories that tell of incest and prohibited intercourse. These wrong marriages are known as *wadji*, and are relatively common where the sub-section organization of kinship occurs in larger communities.

Thus in the course of their lives a married couple, at their own inclination, and with the full knowledge of the other partner, may have sexual relations with a number of classificatory husbands or wives. This conduct is not viewed as either promiscuous or adulterous, nor does it necessarily impair happy marital relations. Only on rare occasions do legalized extramarital relations affect the parents' attachments to their children, or cause family instability. But excessive promiscuity can affect the stability of a marriage, as does elopement and abduction. These affairs, however, must not be carried out blatantly. Assignations must therefore be carried out in secret. It follows from these accounts that sexual jealousy, though it can exist when marital relationships are sometimes tested, does not exist to the same extent as it might in more monogamous communities.

Another little-known aspect of Aboriginal social behaviour involves polygamous marriage. In the Central Desert region these marriages are common, even today. Up to five wives, and sometimes in excess of twenty, are recorded in some tribes. A polygamous marriage is not always the prerogative of a powerful man, or one of unusual prestige, but is usually the result of personal preference. Quite often many of these wives have been 'passed on' to a man after the death of a brother or uncle, or as a result of a number of promised wives having been arranged for him. These marriages are usually happy and, broadly speaking, there is little rivalry or sexual jealousy displayed by the wives. Since marriage is the desired and recognized goal of everyone, men and women, an unmarried widow is quickly absorbed into a kin-accepted marriage at the death of her husband. Even old unmarried men are looked upon as 'queer or unsexed' or suffering from abnormal sexual tendencies.[3]

This does not mean that the status of women is any way inferior, either as a single or as a married person. She, like her male counterpart, is allowed a great deal of sexual freedom within traditional kinship patterns, and is rarely opposed to the duties surrounding marriage or betrothal. She is neither a chattel to her husband nor economically dependent. Her tribal status is oriented to her procreative ability − a status clearly recognized by men. Her true role becomes clear only when it is acknowledged how important she is in rituals, when natural fertility becomes the object of ceremonial event. For it must be remembered that all Aboriginal sexual behaviour, except promiscuity, is based upon mythic approval. The exploits of

Sky Heroes and mythic beings create the patterns of behaviour by which men and women conduct their sex lives.

Among the Aranda tribes of Central Australia, when a girl has reached marriageable age, she is subjected to an operation known as *Atna-ariltha-kuma* (*atna* = vulva; *kuma* = cut). This ceremony is similar to circumcision among boys. As soon as the operation has been performed by a tribal member ritually unaffiliated to her, the girl is led back to the corroboree ground where her head is decorated and her body painted with a mixture of fat and red ochre. Then she is led back to camp and, the following day, with her intended husband's permission, she is sent to have intercourse with the men who performed the operation. Under normal circumstances, these men would not have been allowed to have sexual contact with the girl. Nevertheless it is clear that normal taboo restrictions are put aside during the deflowering ceremony. Prior to her formal marriage to her husband the girl becomes available to men normally forbidden to her, perhaps as a way of alleviating the social tensions that might exist where sex taboo prevails. In any event, ritual prostitution of this nature does not in any way affect the girl's subsequent status, either as a wife or member of her tribe.[4]

Communal prostitution extends to granting sexual favours in return for payment for tobacco, food and clothing. On Goulburn Island, for example, the women are known to go out hunting, aware that they are being followed by young men. At an agreed meeting place, the couples engage in coitus publicly and gifts are given by the young men as a form of payment. On occasions one girl might find herself sexually partnered by a number of young men. She might copulate with one after another in the presence of all, or she may take one at a time aside until everyone is satisfied. It is said that some women are not satisfied until they have experienced a number of ejaculations – one insertion being too 'quick' for them to enjoy intercourse completely. Among certain of the more licentious women their prestige is enhanced by being able to boast of the number of men they have had during one night. Gossip songs often address sexual prowess among women in the following manner: 'How many men can you take before you get tired?' 'Why, I had so many, one after the other, and I could have taken more. My thighs and vagina are strong – see, even after washing myself, I still drip juices.'[5] Perhaps there is some exaggeration in these remarks; though they do indicate women's pride in perfecting the art of love so that they, and their partners, might enjoy it as much as possible. Sexual athleticism is as much a part of the Aborigine's perspective of human relations as any other display of physical or ceremonial prowess.

## LOVE RITUALS

Where sexual activity finds its true dimension is in the realm of ritual or sacred love. Here, indeed, Aborigines explore a form of Tantric rite which enables them to participate in what Tantric texts term *maithuna*, or union, and what the Aborigines regard as *maraian* (that is sacred). The Kunapipi rites of Northern Australia are a significant example of ritualized sexual activity devoted to the celebration of the 'Old Woman' or the concept of the Great Mother. The Kunapipi cult, though a relatively recent form of religious expression said to have been adapted from Macassan myths by way of contact with island traders from the north, nevertheless incorporates much older myth material associated with the Rainbow Snake.

The Kunapipi cult is a part of a group of ceremonial cycles which celebrate the lives of the principal Sky Heroes of the Arnhem Land region. These include the Waugeluk Sisters, who are swallowed by the Rainbow Snake, as well as Djanggawul, a spirit-being who possessed a huge penis and who regularly had sexual contact with his sisters in order to keep them pregnant. According to myth, Djanggawul arrived in northeast Arnhem Land at the time of the Dreaming from Bralku, the Land of the Dead. As they journeyed about the land he used to lift their clitori to one side, put his hand into their uteri, remove numerous children of both sexes and so populate the earth. The perpetual pregnancy of the sisters as a result of ritual incest echoes the self-engendering principle of the world creator, whether it be a formalized God or a mythic being. Incest, while it might not be practised by men and women, is nevertheless considered important to the creation of the world. For it is only out of unity that duality comes into being.

However, the Kunapipi cult, deals with two important concepts: that of the Great Mother (uterus) and the Rainbow Snake (penis). She is the symbol of the productive qualities of the earth, the eternal replenisher of human, animal and natural resources. Sometimes she appears as two sisters or as her own two daughters, both exotic and beautiful, who represent the ideal of young womanhood. As the Original Mother she is responsible for the birth of all human totems, so the principle of identification, indeed human delineation, is an essential part of her character. She is also responsible for sending out the spirits of all natural species from season to season. Though in this she does not act entirely alone. Her ritual association with the Rainbow Serpent, the symbolic penis, ensures that duality is acknowledged.[6]

Her ceremony and ritual embodies the principle of return to the womb and subsequent rebirth, refreshed and renewed. The ceremonial ground or 'ring place' (nonggaru) is a symbolic representation of the uterus into which each man must enter during the rites. The Great Mother, Kunapipi, allows her neophytes to leave once they have been ritually cleansed. Such a cleansing usually involves the ceremonial exchange of wives in order to have sexual intercourse. Thus the fertility of all species, including humankind, is stimulated to the point where the world is able to renew itself. It is significant that among the Yirrkalla people Kunapipi means 'whiste-cock' or sub-incised penis. It is also known as wirii which means 'incisure'. The incised penis symbolizes the Great Snake and the incisure itself the uterus of the Great Woman, Kunapipi. Symbolically male and female members become one, thus affirming the essential unitary nature of the cult.

As indicated earlier, the Kunapipi myth cycle has been grafted onto indigenous mythic material, probably the story of the Waugeluk Sisters themselves. This story relates how the two sisters emerged from the sea at the mouth of the Roper River along with their mother, Kunapipi. They then travelled north, carrying with them knowledge of ritual and fertility. Both of them were pregnant. In the country known as Ilapidji one child was born. The child, Toortoo, was left there when the sisters moved on.

The sisters later camped by a billabong. Here they hunted

various animals and brought them back to the clearing. But each time they tried to cook one of them over a fire, the animals revived and ran away. Hungry after their ordeal, the sisters lay down to sleep. A storm blew up, soaking them where they lay. So one of the sisters decided to dance the Kunapipi dance in the hope of halting the rain. In the end she too lay down to sleep.

Here the blood from the sister who had recently given birth seeped into the waterhole. The Rainbow Snake, Wittee, smelt the blood from his haven at the bottom of the pool and decided to investigate. He rose up out of his coils and swallowed the sisters whole. Feeling sleepy after his meal, Wittee lay down. In his dreams he heard a voice telling him that perhaps he had eaten his sisters. So the next morning he vomited them both up. When they began to stir, he had second thoughts and decided to kill them. He broke their bones and swallowed them once more.

Later, when Wittee was asked by another snake what he had eaten, he lied, telling him that he had eaten a kangaroo. But the snake did not believe him. Eventually Wittee admitted that he had eaten the Waugeluk Sisters. When asked to bring them up again, he refused, saying: 'I can't give these two up. They are *maraian*, my sacred knowledge.' As an act of penance, however, he cut a vein in his arm and allowed blood to spurt out.

From then on, whenever Wittee spoke, he knew it was the two sisters speaking out of his mouth. 'We are here now,' the sisters said, 'the Snake has eaten us. We are the maraian, the sacred knowledge of Wittee. Our spirits talk through him for another country.' When Wittee spoke to his people he always spoke as one with the spirits of the two sisters. 'I give you my ceremonies', he announced. He then went into a big cave, and placed a big stone over the entrance so that he could never come out again.[7]

The story highlights the fact that originally it was women who possessed the sacred knowledge pertaining to culture and religion. The Rainbow Snake's act of cannibalism suggests that men finally took possession of it for themselves, preserving in consequence doctrinal dominance when it came to tribal law. Kunapipi's fertility, her ability to make all things, became the possession of men, not as act but as knowledge. From hence-forth it was men who performed the rites in accordance with the sacred law stolen from women. They in turn orchestrated the great round of ceremonies known today as the Kunapipi songs. It is clear that Kunapipi is 'Queen of the World', the eternal symbol of nature in her abundance. The Great Snake's role, on the other hand, is one of insemination, the principle of conception, the embodiment of the intellectual idea which presages incarnation and birth. What the Great Snake 'stole' from the sisters, and by proxy from Kunapipi herself, was the germ of culture, the knowledge of how to order survival. Pregnacy, birth, rain, the death of animals and their vivification after contact with fire – these motifs emphasize the essentially fructive nature of the myth and its adherence to all forms of renewal.

These ideas are given expression in the great round of songs and dances associated with what Berndt calls 'the ritual face of love'. Ritual action and eroticism coalesce on the nonggaru ground prior to the monsoon season, with the intention of instigating rain. What transpires is an event which typifies a people whose religious values draw them towards deifying coitus as an expression of sacred love. Men and women become ritual rather than sexual partners as they evoke *knaninja*, the Spirit of Sex, that mythic being with the power to transform human emotions into manifold expressions of unity. He alone makes men and women succumb to the allure of what in Hindu mythology is known as *Maksha*, liberation. The pursuit of sexual pleasure under the aegis of ritual renewal ensures them of a transformative experience. They alone bear the responsibility for the arrival of the monsoon rains as they enact the *frisson* of opposites.

The Rose River Cycle[8] of songs from north-eastern Arnhem Land celebrates this theme of fertility. A series of twenty-six songs, it speaks of the encounter between the men from Rose River, Blue Mud Bay and other clans of the region, with the object of ritual defloration of inland girls. The girls are willing participants in the event, of course, as they too acknowledge their role in bringing on the wet season. The song cycle explores in detail the lineage of the clans, the languages they speak, the preparations required in order to perform the dances, the building of the nonggaru, or 'ring place', along with insistent sexual allusions designed to intensify the eroticism of the event for the participants. As rain clouds appear in the sky, so the participants draw towards a ritual climax of their own. All life is drawn into this web of fecundity, so that by the time the morning pigeon calls, and mist rises through the spider threads, the entire world has renewed itself as a gesture of consubstantiation with the Earth Mother, Kunapipi. The cries of the Rose River boys and the girls from the inland are indistinguishable from the squeal of marsupial rats and the call of birds. Thus men and women, animals, birds and insects, fire and rain – all are conjoined and are liberated from the threat of drought through the act of sacred love.

The songs themselves are filled with detail, and to our way of thinking are sometimes repetitious. But this is the nature of ritual: building slowly, and with care for detail, towards an eventual apotheosis. In that sense, they parallel the sexual act itself. Thus, in the first song, we hear:

> They are always there, men chipping at wooden boomerangs:
> Men of the Rose River Clans, of the barramundi and catfish, . . .
> Chips of wood fly out, from shaping the wooden
> boomerangs . . .
> They are always there, women moving their buttocks . . .
> Men chipping and shaping boomerangs, flattening their
> sides . . .
> They think of the nonggaru place, of the sacred ground . . .
> They are always there, men of the southern tribes:
> Clans from the Rose River country, men with sub-incised
> penes . . .
> Clans from the inland bush . . .
> They make the boomerangs, chipping and flattening the sides
> and the defloration point . . .
> Thinking about dancing and rites of the *Kunapipi*.[9]

Already the rhythmical manufacture of boomerangs echoes the licentiousness of the female participants. The boomerang, as symbolic penis, is being prepared for the ritual defloration. Though the theme of fertility is not yet apparent, mention of Kunapipi and defloration provide ample clue to subsequent events.

> Talking quickly like birds, twisting their tongues.

Talking together quickly: hear the sound of their voices those
   people of southern clans!
Twisting their tongues as they talk, speaking slowly in different
   dialects, all the clans together.
In those places at Rose River, among the clumps of bamboo.
The sound drifts over towards the place of the Snake.

Here we are confronted not only with the sexual imagery of
twisting tongues, but with the image of language as seminal
expression. Language, the instrument of purest fecundation, is
identified with the coming together of the clans, of their need
to renew contacts, and of their desire to sound out prospec-
tive sexual partners. Song two intimates co-operation among
the clans by way of language and the ever-present 'moving
buttocks and sub-incised penes'. All the while their chatter
is heard by the Great Snake in her northern manifestation as
the Earth Mother, Kunapipi.

They are sitting there, pounding red ochre,
Those spirits, people of southern clans with sub-incised
   penes . . .
With chest moving, these red-ochre pounders, men of the
   southern clans . . .
For this is the hard red ochre . . .
They sit there, chipping off fragments, preparing paint.
We saw their chest moving, pounding the ochre, men
   of the southern clans . . .
Within the nonggaru, in the vagina, within the sacred blade . . .

While the men prepare and paint the boomerangs for the
defloration ceremony, we sense the intermingling of red ochre
with the idea of phallic 'hardness' and blood, the inevitable
outcome of the defloration process. At this point the women
are sitting in the shade of nonggaru, the sacred shade, the
womb of the Great Mother. By song four they are 'thinking
of ritual intercourse in the sacred shade' and invoking 'the
power of the wind' to summon the Great Snake from the
waterhole.

By song five the sexual imagery has become more intense.
In the nonggaru shade, the men are wielding their boomerangs
as symbolic penises while the women await their ritual
defloration 'standing ready in rows' in the shade. In song
six a frenzy of boomerang throwing is initiated as a reminder

of the movement of cloud and the need to 'impregnate' the sky if it is to yield rain:

> Thus they threw them, towards the place of the Snake, the
>   place of the Crab, the place of the Catfish . . .
> Flying boomerangs, from the spirit people, clan of the
>   paperbark saplings, with heaving chests . . .
> Throwing the boomerangs towards Blue Mud Bay, the Vagina
>   place . . .
> Special boomerangs, with flattened sides, and points made for
>   defloration . . .

Songs seven and eight emphasize the significance of the boomerangs as ritual objects relating to the monsoon season. This power of invocation attracts rain. By song nine a world-womb has been constructed out of branches in preparation for the final act of coitus. In the meantime, the actions of all the participants have become concentrated on the need to arouse one another:

> They are building the screen, arranging the branches . . .
> Thinking of women's vaginas, and of coitus.
> They are always there, people with moving buttocks:
> Clans with sub-incised penes, clans of the barramundi . . .
> All the southern clans, assembled together . . .
> Arranging the screen to hide the women within . . .

By song eleven the young girls find themselves transformed into 'sacred girls', *maraian*, their bodies subsumed by the prospect of sacred love and the act of making rain:

> Young girls, painted with red ochre, moving towards
>   the branches screening the shade . . .
> Arranging the girls, ready for defloration, for they are sacred . . .

In song twelve and thirteen sacred love is consumated. The women will, perhaps for the first and only time, enjoy sexual relations with a man normally taboo to them. According to Berndt, the sacredness of the occasion inverts and simultaneously draws a positive advantage from the taboo: coitus between these otherwise taboo relatives is regarded as far more potent from the point of view of fertility than would normally be the case. The sanctity of the occasion intensifies the eroticism, of course, but it also induces a fecund psychological field in which the participants enact their parts.

> They bring close the pointed boomerang, raising her thighs
> onto the hip of a man . . .
> Pushing her down, that young girl smeared with ochre,
>   raising her thighs . . .
> They think of the boomerang with its flattened point . . .
> Pushing her down, that girl, on a man's hips,
>   into the branches . . .
> They bring close the point of the boomerang, into her vulva . . .
> Girls crying out, pierced by the flattened point of the
>   boomerang . . .
> The sound drifts as they cry out from that boomerang . . .
> Sound in the sacred camp, in the nonggaru place
>   among the clumps of bamboo.
> They are copulating together, to the sound of singing
>   with penis erect . . .
> The penis moves slowly, 'talking', as he ejaculates;
> Erect penis copulating, moving forward.
> Semen streams out into the young girl, within
>   the screen of branches . . .
> Copulating among the branches, to the sound of singing . . .
> The penis moves slowly, 'talking', as he ejaculates.
> Semen ejaculating from the erect penis,
> Large penis, entering the young girl.
> Mouth of the penis, penis growing erect:
> Its tip smells of the girl's vaginal juices . . .
> At the place of the Snake, the place of the Rising Penis . . .
> Men of the southern clans, clans of the sub-incision
>   with penes ridged and erect.

Song fourteen describes the women's actions after ritual copulation. By striking their bellies, they hope to dislodge the semen and so bring on rain by this symbolic act. They are termed 'sub-incised' girls for the first time, thus identifying their vaginas (from which flows semen and defloration blood) and the sub-incised penis. Thus the genitals of both men and women become one during the ritual event. Sacred love has unified men and women, distancing them from their inherent sexual duality. To emphasize this unity, the young women are smeared with red ochre as well as their defloration blood prior to leaving the sacred ground. The men also smear themselves, so that both sexes 'look the same'. At this point they are said to be emerging from the Great Mother's womb, reborn fresh and renewed.

> Smearing the young girls, rubbing them all over with red
>   ochre . . .
> Their skin shining, shining from ochre and fat . . .

By song sixteen a transformation has occurred. The clouds are now blood red and yellow tinged, the colour of deflorated women and men's semen. All nature has become identified with ritual coitus, and so is made fecund. The clouds are 'shining all over the country', 'hanging over the barramundi clans', 'blood and ochre shining' in such a way as to make cloud and body indistinguishable from one another.

By song seventeen, the women have returned to camp alone, leaving the men to complete the sub-incision rites, a vital complement to the ceremony. In song eighteen the men prepare the stone blades for cutting the penis. At the same time:

> They think of the rising penis, moving in coitus, ejacu-
>   lating . . .
> Thinking of copulating, and of the penis and tip ring as they
>   sit there flaking the stone . . .
> Calling invocations to running water, to semen ejaculating . . .

Song nineteen describes the operation of sub-incisure whereby the stone blade is used to split the penis open from the tip to the beginning of the ring. This is the prelude for that climactic moment when, in song twenty, ritual defloration, coitus and sub-incision are symbolically manifested in the wet season. Clouds, having been formed from blood, ochre, semen and kangaroo fat, now drift over Rose River and Blue Mud Bay, the black bands in their patterns likened to the breast girdles worn by young girls.

> Clouds rise in the sky, bending down towards the place of the
>   Snake . . .
> Clouds, bending and shaking, crossed by black bands like
>   young girls' breast girdles . . .
> Like boomerangs flung into the clouds, like breast girdles
>   merging together . . .

What follows in song twenty is a powerful poetic rendition of cloud formation. All aspects of the ritual are drawn together at this point in an expression of the coming wet season:

> They rise high into the sky, spreading across, bending down
>   over the place of the Snake . . .
> They stand, indeed, stretching away inland, among
>   the armband bushes, among the clumps of bamboo . . .
> They rise, changing their shapes, with small clouds drifting
>   upwards . . .
> Clouds bending down, reaching across like hands
>   joining together . . .

Song twenty-one introduces the Great Snake in the form of the Lightning Snake as an active participant in the ritual for the first time. The tongue of the Lightning 'flashes along the top of the clouds/making them shine like ochre' as it 'rears its tail, rearing its head quickly up from its hole'. It smells the young girls' blood and blood from the sub-incised penises, and announces:

> 'Here I swallow the blood, and it goes into my belly . . .'
> Snake, with its backbone, flashing the lightning . . .
> Smelling the blood of the young girls, returning to eat.

The spilt blood, the primal offering of the participants to the Rainbow Snake, is designed to ensure his gift of rain. Song twenty-three announces that the wet season is over, and that the grass may be burned in order that the new shoots might come through, thus encouraging game to return. By songs twenty-four and twenty-five the spiders are weaving their webs once more, the marsupial rats are hopping about, the new grass is growing: a sense of nature renewing itself after the wet season is everywhere evident. By songs twenty-six, the rhythm of nature finds itself once more in harmony with men and women, their powers of procreation intermingled in an act of ritual love. The final words conjure up a timeless sense of the order of things, and how this order must be reaffirmed by way of an act of lovemaking which for once transcends tribal taboos, so partaking of the divine disorder lying beneath the surface of manifestation.

> The Morning Pigeon is calling . . .
> Bird, its voice like the speech of those clans, people who talk
>   like birds.

109

Its cries sound through the haze, through the mist of smoke
and of spider-threads ...
Bird, ruffling its feathers and crying ...
In that sacred camp, in the place, of nonggaru.
It flies low, touching the branches of the nonggaru
of the armband bushes.
Its cry sounds through the mist, like the speech of the southern
clans, clans of the sub-incision ...
Its cry echoing out, as it enters its nest.

Here we have the final expression of the Kunapipi rites, dedicated as they are to the conjoining of Aborigines with nature. The erotic content of the rituals highlights the desire on the part of Aborigines to imitate the role of nature as procreator, as renewer of life. Sacred love rites are designed to ensure a concentration of energy in this process. By breaking laws of taboo with regard to sexual partnerships, Aborigines place themselves outside the field of conventional morality, and so align themselves with the wilder laws of nature. It is important to understand that by balancing tribal law against the laws of nature Aborigines are able to transform normal lovemaking activity into a powerful force which derives its potency from that indefinable area of human experience where emotions are gripped by an imperative more substantive than any derived from tribal law.

This is why sacred love has a place within the context of Aboriginal society. While it might be treated circumspectly at one level, at another it has an important role to play. Ritually breaking kinship laws prior to the monsoon season allows Aborigines the opportunity to explore human relationships that might otherwise be closed to them. This softens the rigidity of tribal law and so makes it possible for sexual partners to derive pleasure from standing outside this law at least once in their lifetime. More importantly, perhaps, sacred love allows Aborigines to transform their bodies into a symbolic field whereby they are able to echo the procreative power of nature. By doing so, they are able to draw closer to the realm of the Dreaming where all true archetypes reside. Invoking the monsoon rains through the act of group sexual play ensures that nature's pageant achieves the full status of a sacred marriage between man and those earthly forces which

govern the conduct of terrestrial occurences. Only through
the Kunapipi ceremonies can men and women abandon their
social identity for a short while and participate more fully
in this event. Rain, blood, lightning, cloud, ritual wounding,
vaginal juices, semen, birds, animals, insects and vegetation –
all these elements are drawn together to form a web of reality
which transcends all others. The world is made new again,
exhausted energies are revivified, and thus that timeless order
within nature is reaffirmed once more for the benefit of all
living creatures.

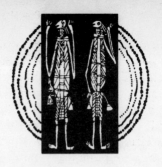

# 8 · THE YELLOW OCHRE DANCE

For the Aboriginal people death is not a terminal condition but a transcendent rite. Although ritual and mortuary practice surrounding death may vary considerably throughout the country, in nearly all cases the spirit's act of quitting the body is not considered to be a mark of cessation of being. Whether a body is buried in the earth or on an aerial platform, whether it is laid flat or positioned upright with its knees doubled up against its chin in a grave, emphasis is placed upon not *where* a person is buried so much as *how* and *when* his or her spirit will depart safely to the Realm of the Dead. This is because a person's death, though a natural event in one sense, is a metaphysical event in another. He or she, whether adult or child, invariably dies not because of old age or disease, but because of the intercession of some outside agent, either in the form of a breach of religious taboo or because of an untoward act of sorcery.

Thus death is regarded as a significant transformative event in the life of both family and tribal community. Natural death is but a precondition to the reintegration of the spiritual being into the rich ancestral reservoir known as the Dreaming. When a person approaches old age, he or she increasingly discusses the possibility of death and makes preparations for it. This includes the passing on of religious knowledge, and ensuring that sacred songs and stories are correctly distributed within the clan prior to death. One old man who considered that all preparations had been completed to his satisfaction in this matter regarded himself, from that point on, as 'really dead', and so merely awaiting to join the Ancestors.[1]

Acknowledging one's impending death is one way of taking responsibility for it, therefore avoiding the repercussions of blaming someone else. By stating that one is ready to die, and as a result bearing no one any feeling of ill will, means that a person has control over his own death. In contrast, Aborigines often argue that Europeans have no foreknowledge of death, and are unable to prepare for it; whereas Aborigines are able to communicate with the Sky Heroes when they are about to die, often drawing from them a presentiment of the exact time and place of death. The songs a dying person hears, though designed to 'make a person happy', are also intercessionary devices with the Sky Heroes. A dying man is said to make motions imitating his totemic animal. When his relatives sing the song of the whale, for example, he kicks to simulate the movement of the whale's body at sea. In this way he is 'becoming like his totem'. The dying man is able to merge with his 'other life' to the point where his immediate physical death loses some of its importance. Living on in his totem, therefore, assures him (or her) of an abiding existence outside the constraints of the body.

### THE TRANSFORMATION OF THE SOUL

Intrinsic to the death of the individual is the smooth egress of two souls – or more properly, two dimensions of the soul – from the body. Known among the Yolngu people of north-east Arnhemland as the *birrimbirr* and *mokuy* spirits, such dimensions of the soul correspond analogically to the *ba* and *ka* birds of Egyptian mortuary rite[2] or *Yin* and *Yang* in Chinese cosmology. The mokuy spirit is said to exist independently of the world-creating Sky Heroes of the Dreaming. After a person dies, the mokuy soul returns to that part of the clan's territory where all mokuy spirits live. Such areas of land are known as mokuy, and are generally localized, in contrast to the Dreaming tracks of Sky Heroes which are everywhere.

Unlike the Sky Heroes, the mokuy are often capricious and harmful to humankind. They sometimes cause trouble among relatives and even cause injury or death to anyone implicated in the person's death.

On the other hand, the birrimbirr soul is a more complex concept, denoting a person's spiritual existence in the Dreaming. One aspect of it relates to the animating spirit (totem) effective in a person's conception. The birrimbirr, too, is said to return to clan land, though not in a localized sense, there to be reincorporated into the reservoir of djang (supernatural power) associated with that place. While many myths might tell of how souls travel to the Realm of the Dead, climbing up a possum fur string to be transformed into stars in the Milky Way, the essence of the birrimbirr spirit merges with the more generalized power of the Sky Heroes, where it becomes immanent in the sacred objects of the tribe. This aspect of the soul is also associated with the bones of the deceased, since it is the bones that survive death, later to become reincorporated into the land as djang when they are finally buried.

For Aborigines the dual aspect of soul is thus able to embrace the complexity of being at the time of death. Just as a person is himself and his totem in life; so in death his spirit splits into what might be termed complementary opposites. The need for one aspect of being to return to the 'land that made him' reinforces an Aborigine's deep sense of nostalgia for his piece of earth. But it is important for another aspect, the more malign element (mokuy), of a man's being also to be reintegrated. The whole man is therefore safely able to pass over into the Beyond, both in the good and the bad sense, so that no part of him remains 'in life' to trouble those left behind. Furthermore, having control of his or her death, a person is able to ensure that the transition of both birrimbirr and mokuy is completed correctly. The songs and the dances, the painting of the coffin with the exact designs, the construction among northern tribes of sand sculptures in honour of the dead – all these are a vital part of the process of expediting the soul to its true home in the Dreaming. This is done during the mortuary ceremonies, of which the Yellow Ochre dance fulfils an important role of reintegration.

The burial ceremony and the accompanying dances are

114

designed to aid the birrimbirr soul's return to the Dreaming. They are also designed to drive away the mokuy spirit, and so eliminate the prospect of pollution to those who remain behind. As the spirit is said to rise 'like smoke' from the fire into the sky, where it forms, or joins, rain clouds drifting across to the spirit home of the deceased,[3] there is a close association between the idea that the spirit may travel in water, sometimes flowing in streams across the countryside from one tribal well to another. This primordial link with the Rainbow Snake is further enhanced by the belief in underground connections; though it is also conceded that the spirit might manifest itself in the form of birds, white cockatoos, for example – or indeed shooting stars. Summoning up Sky Heroes to guide the spirit of the deceased back to the Dreaming is central to the rituals. The songs are designed to 'give power to the body' in order to aid the spirit's journey.

## THE DEATH RITES

The first phase of the ceremony at the death of an individual involves the singing of songs beside the body. While this is occurring, a shade is built to house the coffin where it has been constructed and ritually painted. Many of the songs contain major symbols of death. The mangrove tree, eaten through by worms, is a popular symbol of a dead body. In contrast, the tide marks made by a king tide represent the cleansing of the ground and the erasing of all physical evidence of the deceased, much as the waves wash away footprints to leave the sand smooth and clean once more. In the case of the Yolngu people who live by the sea, freshwater and saltwater songs are used should the birrimbirr decide to take either a land or sea route home. These songs form an adjunct to the business of building a shade so that it might 'look beautiful for the body'. Rolls of cloth are used to cover the area, and to a certain extent contain the smell should it become too offensive.

Painting the coffin, however, constitutes the single most important aspect of the ceremony. For the coffin acts as a message to the spirits of previously deceased relatives, asking them to collect the dead person's spirit and guide it back to the clan well.[4] It acts as an immediate point of contact between the spirit and the Sky Heroes, providing a vehicle by which the mortuary drama is raised from the profane to the celestial sphere. The coffin paintings arm the spirit with a special power which protect it after death. Acting as a talismanic device, each painting helps the spirit of the deceased on his journey to the Dreaming. As one old man related, 'When he dies we paint the lid of the coffin. We give these sacred paintings to him [the deceased] so he'll take them with him when he becomes a spirit, when his old dead relatives come close to him and take him to his *sacred land*' [author's italics].[5] Inspired by the Sky Heroes themselves, such paintings are considered to be more ritually potent than either the dances or the songs, probably because they were not devised by human hands.[6] In any event, the paintings on the coffin are iconographic expressions of the deceased's relationship to his country, and to the Dreaming itself. By the fourth day, and after the painting is completed, it is time for the performance of the Yellow Ochre dance.

Before the dance begins, however, the men paint themselves and then assemble behind the shade where the body lies. They paint themselves with yellow ochre, a symbol of the deceased's body and also of the clan's blood link with the Dreaming ancestors. It is, in a sense, a spiritual essence which is said to strengthen the blood of the participants. Digging up yellow ochre represents a search for the dead body, and placing it in the coffin. As one informant remarked, 'The yellow ochre represents the body. Just as a person gets ochre and places it in a dilly bag, so we put the body [in the coffin]. Opening up, digging the ground, we get the body just like yellow ochre.'[7] The dance reflects the opening up of the shade so that the body can be formally placed in the coffin.

The dance is performed with controlled aggression. Muscles are tensed, and digging sticks thrust like spears into the ground in front of the shade. All the negative aspects of death, those feelings of anger and frustration generated by the event, are brought into focus so that the 'dark angel' (the mokuy spirit)[8] is driven away. Fires are lit also, and loud noises made to encourage the mokuy's flight. By these actions the embodiment of the deceased's material existence in the form of the mokuy is driven off, in order that the man's true spirit, his birrimbirr soul, is allowed to depart in safety. As one informant remarked:

> Before the body had been laid to rest in the coffin, you are very angry. You feel wild, you break down, you are against the songs, the body, everything. If you just use your feelings then you are against the box or against the people – you must bite the dilly bag, hold yourself, make yourself still and you'll be settled down. But if you suspect someone has caused the death – then everybody bites the dilly bag, that's your connection, your power up from the dilly bag. You put into your mind all the thoughts, and you connect everything to your power.[9]

The dilly bag filled with yellow ochre becomes a symbol of resolve, a way of empowering a dancer with courage to take vengeance on the suspected perpetrator of the death. This is largely a ritualistic gesture used to defy the odds and relieve frustration, so to speak, and rarely results in someone seeking out another for the purpose of causing harm. The Yellow Ochre ceremony prepares the participants for the trauma of the body being placed in the coffin for the last time. With the mokuy spirit driven off and the birrimbirr soul successfully on its way to clan territory, the moment is essentially cathartic. All the emotions of grief and aggressiveness are brought under control by the participants.

Finally, when the Yellow Ochre dance is completed, the cover over the entrance to the shade is removed. The coffin is then brought from the hut, where it has lain during the dance, accompanied by dancers who kick up dust and drag sticks along the ground. These actions symbolize the floodwaters of the inland rivers buffeting the coffin (implicitly containing the body) on its way to the sea during the wet season. Such an image is regarded as a major symbol of birth and death. Songs detailing the actions of fish bursting out of fish traps, or dragging a harpoon through the water all signify the fish's desire to be free from containment and the threat of death. Thus the feeling of 'breaking free' from earthly attachments is reiterated in both dance and song. Bodily decay as symbolized by the mangrove trees, hollow logs floating down rivers as symbols of coffins – such images become appropriate reflections of disintegration and dispersal of dead or decaying materials.

Ultimately the deceased's spirit is travelling towards the sea, the Ocean of Remembrance, where all souls are regenerated.

A link is also made between the coffin and snakes. Indeed, after the body has been placed in the coffin, snakes take over as the main symbolic agency for transferring the spirit of the deceased to its clan territory. Conceptually linked to floodwaters, the Rainbow Snake swims up river ahead of the coffin, tasting the water as it goes. When it finally tastes fresh water and swallows it, the Snake is said to be swallowing the spirit of the deceased. One informant remarks, 'If he [the Snake] feels the water tasting good, he drinks the box [coffin].' Much of the singing and dancing at this stage reflects the actions of the Ancestral Snake (that is, the Rainbow Snake) as it absorbs the spirit of the deceased, taking it to its bosom.

In the cool of the evening the coffin is then transported to the burial site. All the while songs recount the power names of the tide and the mangrove tree ancestor. At the graveside, men of the mother crocodile clan dance energetically around the mound of earth. The coffin is then lowered into the grave, and the crocodile dancers proceed to flick earth into the hole. The final phase of the ceremony is accompanied by the lighting of numerous fires. The smoke produced by these fires is said to 'cover up the funeral' – that is, it acts as a purifying agent for both participants and sacred objects used in the ceremony. The use of fire, and the symbolism of the crocodile in association with the deceased's body, also suggests the idea of an 'egg' (body) being laid to rest in the 'nest' of a crocodile where the prospect of rebirth in assured by the heat of the 'fire' (sun).

The formal aspects of burial are now complete. But the ritual aspects continue beyond this point to include the eventual exhuming of the body months, or sometimes years, later. The bones are cleaned and ochred, before being placed in a bark pouch or hollow log so that they might be easily transported. In this way they can be carried about by relatives until it is felt that the birrimbirr spirit has finally reached home. The bones are either crushed and scattered about clan territory, or they are placed in a cave sacred to the clan.[10] The pilgrimage is finally over. The remains of the deceased are reintegrated with his country in preparation for the process of reincarnation to begin all over again.

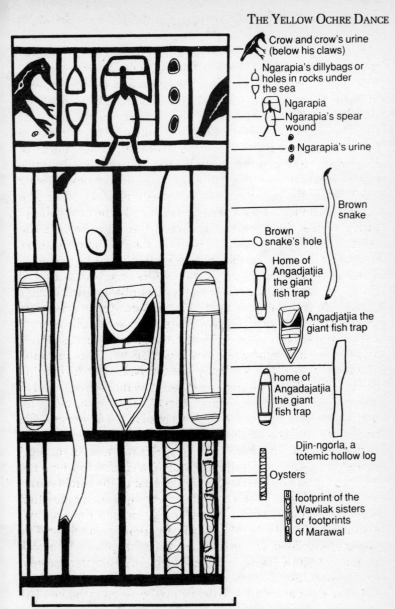

Crow and crow's urine (below his claws)

Ngarapia's dillybags or holes in rocks under the sea

Ngarapia

Ngarapia's spear wound

Ngarapia's urine

Brown snake

Brown snake's hole

Home of Angadjatjia the giant fish trap

Angadjatjia the giant fish trap

home of Angadajatjia the giant fish trap

Djin-ngorla, a totemic hollow log

Oysters

footprint of the Wawilak sisters or footprints of Marawal

Fig. 10   Sketch of the ornamental *dupun* showing the subjects and their dispositions, but omitting the cross-hatching (*rrarak*) which the men decided could not be seen. (Courtesy of Margaret Clunies Ross and L. R. Hiatt, from their article 'Sand sculpture at Gidjingali burial rite'.)

Of course, the ritual of burial varies throughout Australia. But the essential rites and songs, themselves only contingent realities, are repeated in one form or another. Whether the apertures on the body are all sewn up, or hair removed prior to burial; these are of less importance than is the overall belief in the need for the spirits to return to their homeland. Even canoe burial among inland river tribes was not uncommon in the past. Among the Arunta of Central Australia the practice was to seat the corpse in a round hole, knees drawn up to the chin. The hole was then filled in to form a mound with a depression on one side facing the deceased's totemic territory, specifically the sacred place associated with his or her conception. This makes it possible for *ulthana*, or spirit, to quit the body and finally join its 'spirit double' or *arumburinga* who lived in the Dreaming site *(Nanja).*[11]

However much ritual details might vary, the essential motifs remain the same. The dual aspects of the soul must be released from the prison of the flesh in order to make the journey home to clan territory. But this does not mean that the deceased's memory diminishes as time goes by. Among the Gidjingali people of Arnhemland, for example, a dead person's bones are often placed in a hollowed out pole known as a *dupun*. This ornamental pole, usually decorated with motifs sacred to clan members of the deceased, becomes a permanent icon of family totemic associations, as well as mythological material (see Figure 10). On Bathurst Island among the Tiwi people, these poles are known as *pukamani*, and can be seen standing in groups about a clearing. They in turn form a part of a remarkable sand sculpture ceremony known as a *larrakan* among the Gidjingali.[12]

Sand sculpture is a form of mortuary art. Every design represents totemic affiliations and the stories associated with each one. In sand sculpture 1 (see Figure 11), known as Wudjal, we see the home of porpoise. He dives at the first basin-like hollow at the eastern end of the sand sculpture, swims along the central channel, surfaces at the middle hollow and then dives again, finally surfacing at the hollow at the western end of the sculpture. This story finds its variants in sculptures 2 and 3 which explore the supernatural landscape connected with the deceased father's clan. Sand sculpture 4 is said to have been originally a man who was speared by a group of warriors. Though fierce and dangerous, he was transformed after death into a large black rock, shaped like a man, which can be seen today off the coast. The rock has a hole in it through which the sea spurts. This hole represents the man's body wound.

Each sculpture reinforces the relationship between the deceased and clan territory, between his spirit and the metaphysical landscape of his tribe. For the living, they offer an opportunity to partake of a unique form of cleansing in the company of the deceased. This is usually done during a washing ceremony (*ngarra*) which is performed in the 'well' of one of these sand sculptures. Members of the deceased's clan take turns to sit at the centre of such a sand spring while the ceremonial leader pours water over them, calling out 'power names' (*bundurr*) of the clan and its country. After the ceremonial washing, most people smear red ochre over their

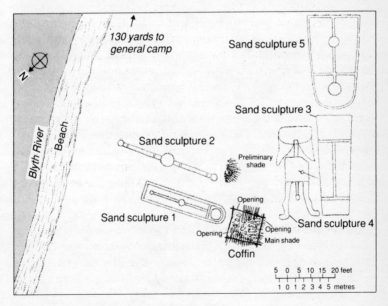

Fig. 11  Sketch of the ceremonial ground at a *dupun* mortuary rite, showing the location of sand sculptures 1–5. (Courtesy of Margaret Clunies Ross and L. R. Hiatt, from their article 'Sand sculpture at Gidjingali burial rite'.)

bodies as a sign that they have been cleansed. All this is done in the vicinity of the coffin pole which is positioned near the sand sculptures. In such a way the deceased's spirit is drawn back into the web of the living, exercising his metaphysical power from beyond the grave.[13]

Among the Arunta of Central Australia, the practice of formally burying the arm bone of someone who had died and who had been the subject of earlier mortuary ceremonies, took on picturesque detail according to observers during the early part of this century.[14] Ten men, their bodies elaborately decorated with feather down in red, yellow and white, straddled a trench in the earth of about 1 ft deep and 20 ft in length. Each man clasped his hands above his head. Nearby a painting of the deceased's totem decorated the earth. The women of the tribe approached and proceeded to crawl along the trench under the men's outstretched legs, the last one carrying a bark pouch containing the arm bone of the deceased. This was snatched away from the woman as she rose to her feet and carried off to where an old man, armed with a stone axe, stood beside a small pit in the ground. The pit lay near the sand painting of the deceased's totem. Immediately the arm bone was shattered into pieces and buried in the pit under a flat stone. In this way

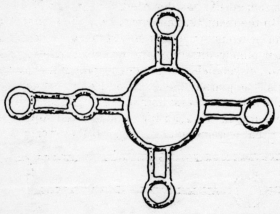

Fig. 12   Liyagalawumirri clan sand sculpture made for a washing ceremony. It represents springs made by the Djang'kawu sisters at Detjirima, Howard Island. (Courtesy of Ian Keen, from his article 'Yolngu sand sculptures in context'.)

the spirit of the deceased was said to 'have gathered unto his totem'. The final act of burial was now complete.

In all cases we are confronted with a finely tuned relationship between the living and the dead, between totemic existence and the bones of the deceased, and between the clan territory and the spirit of the deceased. Aborigines are clearly motivated by a deep attachment to the dead, and a desire to make sure that they reach the Realm of the Dead safely. The 'crossing over', whether by way of a ritual coffin voyage, as among the Yolngu, or by way of a trench walk, as among the Arunta, is accompanied by elaborate ceremonies designed to ensure that a safe haven is reached. The use of sand sculpture and sand paintings, mortuary poles and bark pouches provide a body of material to elucidate symbolic identity, and to ground the dead person in the mythic drama of his or her people. At no time is the deceased anonymous; indeed his or her cultural identity is ritually affirmed at every stage of the mortuary ceremony. This means that the deceased goes to his Maker shorn only of his physical body, which in turn is the subject of careful appraisal by the living after the spirit's departure. His (or her) bones become cultural as well as spiritual artefacts, relics for the living to identify with once their partner in life has departed. The power of these relics resides in the djang that emanates from them after death.

A man or woman acquires new status after death. Though no longer among the living, he or she is able to exercise a significant psychological influence upon relatives and clan members. The journey the deceased makes as a dual spirit to the Realm of the Dead is synonymous with the journey all men and women make through life, aided by the supportive staff of rite, ritual, ceremony and song. All these form the canon

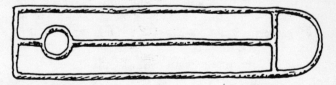

Fig. 13   Gamalangga clan sand sculpture made for a washing ceremony. (Courtesy of Ian Keen, from his article 'Yolngu sand sculpture in context'.)

of belief to which every Aborigine is committed by the very act of being. Life and death are represented by the duality of spirit, the mokuy and the birrimbirr, the physical and the spiritual. Each counterbalances the other. No physical life can be eternal, nor can any death be more than a transitionary state. Aboriginal people are always aware that their existence is in response to the particular action of spiritual forces outside their control. These forces may be anthropomorphized, they may even be granted Sky Hero status; but in the end they are recognized for what they are: the workings of the Divine Spirit which is beyond the comprehension of humankind.

The bond between the living and the dead among Aborigines suggests an unfamiliar spiritual perspective to many who might regard death as something abhorrent. Yet it is clear these people have drawn their knowledge of it from an ancient source – a source perhaps inspired by real contact with the otherworld in the distant past. This is not to say that Aborigines indulged in occult practices, seemingly so popular during our time; rather, being in possession of a more pristine view of the various conditions of existence, they were able to detect subtle nuances in the process of death and decay, in keeping with a deep spiritual understanding. The need to perform elaborate mortuary ceremonies, sometimes lasting many years, must seem fully justified in the context of such extensive knowledge about the life of the spirit after material death.

The essential feature of all Aboriginal mortuary practice is a desire for the individual spirit to return to that deep reservoir of Spirit. This is achieved by way of acknowledging the role of the earth as a mediator between man and the Creator. For all Aborigines the earth embodies what may be called chthonic gnosis – Earth wisdom – a metaphysical repertoire of ideas, emotions, feelings and intuitions that, taken as a whole, defy all rational analysis. This is as it should be. The modern penchant for the quantification and exploitation of material phenomena can be no substitute, ultimately, for the insight and well-being derived by human beings from the *quality* of their environment. The earth and, by implication, humankind's presence on it and subsequent return to it after the life process has been exhausted, requires formal recognition of its role. At this point the Yellow Ochre dance becomes a gesture of unity, a mark of esteem, a recognition of how important the earth is in the drama of life and death. It is by way of celebration that Aborigines smooth over the disjuncture that death *appears* to present, reconciling themselves at once to the eternal mystery of existence.

In the end, the role of death among Aborigines is one of healing. All rite and ritual is directed towards binding the spirit to the body, making them one, a whole, and then allowing them to separate without rupture. Life in its contingency supports the existence of a celestial landscape, a landscape made up of an all-pervading spiritual reality which underpins the cosmos. At the time of death this relationship is brought into sharp relief and acknowledged, making it possible for Aborigines themselves to join with the Sky Heroes, those invisible spirit entities who orchestrate these spiritual forces, in serving notice that the universe is indeed one rich and undivided whole.

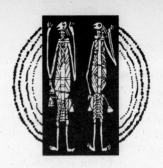

# NOTES

CHAPTER 1

1. Josephine Flood, *Archeology of the Dreamtime*, Collins 1983, pp. 40–8. Also Wilfred Shawcross, *Thirty Thousand Years and More* and *From Earlier Fleets*, Hemisphere, 1978.
2. J. Birdsell, 'The recalibration of a paradigm for the peopling of Great Australia', in *Sunds and Sahul* (edited by J. Allen *et al.*), Academic Press, 1977, pp. 113–67.
3. R.M. and C.H. Berndt, *The World of the First Australians*, Ure Smith, 1977.
4. C.G. Brandl, *The Symbolism of the North-western Australian Zig-zag Design*, Oceania Vol. 42: 3, March 1972. The diagram shown here is derived from this article.
5. C.G. von Brandenstein, *Narratives from the North West of Western Australia in the Ngarluma and Jindjiparndi Languages*, Australian Aboriginal Studies No. 35, Linguistic Series No. 14, 3 Vols, Canberra.
6. Ibid., p. 227.
7. The *Alcheringa* is an Arunta word for the Dreaming, or Time of the Ancestors. There were once well over 200 languages in Aboriginal Australia, so the word would differ accordingly. *Tjukurita* is the Pitjantjara example.
8. James Cowan, *Starlight's Trail*, Doubleday, 1985.
9. Roland Robinson, *Aboriginal Myths and Legends*, Sun Books, 1966.
10. Ludwig Wittgenstein, *Tractatus Logico-Philosophicus* (Routledge, 1974), who said, 'there are, indeed, things

that cannot be put into words. They make themselves
manifest. They are what is mystical' (6.522).

11. Henry Corbin, *Spiritual Body and Celestial Earth*, Bollingen Series 41: 2, 1977. Quoting Pierre Deffontaines,
'The Religious Factor in Human Geography: its Force and
its Limits', p. 34, 'On the other hand, when nowadays there
is no question of the "earth" being anything but a "support
for culture" or a "social function", we can measure the
downfall that has befallen the phenomenon of the Earth
as it appears to the socialized consciousness.'
12. C.P. Mountford, *Winbaraku and the Myth of Jarapiri*,
Rigby, 1968.
13. Author's field notes, 1990.

## CHAPTER 2

1. Quoted in *The Mystery of the Serpent* by Hans Leisegang
in *The Mysteries, Papers from the Eranos Yearbooks*,
edited by Joseph Campbell, Bollingen Series XXX, 1978.
2. A.R. Radcliffe-Brown, *The Rainbow-Serpent Myth in Southeast Australia*, Oceania Vol. 1, 1930–31.
3. W.E.H. Stanner, *What Man Got No Dreaming*, ANU Press,
1979.
4. B. Spencer and F. Gillen, *Native Tribes of Central Australia*, MacMillan & Co, 1938.
5. C.G. von Brandenstein, *Aboriginal Ecological Order in the
South-west of Australia*, Oceania Vol. 47: 3.
6. C.P. Mountford, *Aboriginal Conception Beliefs*, Hyland
House, 1981.
7. M.F. Ashley-Montagu, *Coming into Being among Australian
Aborigines*, Routledge & Kegan Paul, 1937.
8. Ibid., p. 26.
9. Compare with 'Eridanus', or the River of Heaven. For the
Akkadians it was regarded as the Great Serpent.
10. Giorgio de Santillana and Hertha von Dechend, *Hamlet's
Mill*, Godine, 1977.
11. Ibid., p. 306.
12. See C.P. Mountford, *Nomads of the Australian Desert*,
Rigby, 1976, where he says, 'the whole sky is turned
over each night by two men, the older and the younger
guardians of the circumcision ceremony . . . who live in
the constellation of Scorpio.'
13. Author's field notes, 1990.

14. See Rolond Robinson's *Aboriginal Myths and Legends*, Sun Books, 1977, pp. 37–43.
15. W. Arndt, *The Dreaming of Kunukban*, Oceania Vol. 35: 4, June 1965.
16. Ibid.
17. A.P. Elkin, *The Rainbow-Serpent Myth in North-west Australia*, Oceania Vol. 1, 1930–31, pp. 349–52.
18. Wittgenstein, 6.52 and 6.521, p. 73.

CHAPTER 3

1. W.E.H. Stanner, *White Man Got No Dreaming*, ANU Press, 1979.
2. B. Spencer and F. Gillen, *Native Tribes of Central Australia*, Macmillan & Co., 1938.
3. C.G. von Brandenstein, *Aboriginal Ecological Order in the South-west of Australia*, Oceania Vol. 47: 3, 1977.
4. A. Lommel, *Die Unambal*, Hamburg, 1952.
5. Ashley Montagu, *Coming into Being among the Australian Aborigines*, Routledge & Kegan Paul, 1937.
6. R.M. and C.H. Berndt, *The World of the First Australians*, Ure Smith, 1977.
7. T.G.H. Strehlow, *Aranda Traditions*, Melbourne University Press, 1947.
8. Ibid., pp. 133–4.
9. Ibid., pp. 130–1.
10. Author's field notes.
11. Ibid., p. 15.
12. Quoted from Simone Weil, *First and Last Notebooks*, Oxford University Press, 1970. 'homo naturae parendo imperat omnia serviliter pro dominatione.'

CHAPTER 4

1. B. Spencer and F. Gillen, *Native Tribes of Central Australia*, Macmillan & Co., 1938.
2. Ibid., pp. 213–18.
3. T.G.H. Strehlow, *Aranda Traditions*, Melbourne University Press, 1947.
4. Ibid., p. 106.
5. Ibid., p. 260.

6. The *Wandjina* is an important spirit-being of the Kimberley region in Northwest Australia. Reminiscent of a cloud, he possesses large eyes, an aureole of lightning, mist-like shoulders (depicting what is 'beyond our understanding') but without a mouth. This is because he has 'said all' at the time of the Dreaming (compare with, 'In the beginning was the Word', John 1: 1). Among the tribes of the northwest, Wandjinas are responsible for both the law and rain. They are intimately connected with the Rainbow Snake.

7. See my *Mysteries of the Dreaming* (Prism Press, 1989), where the concept of the open-air cathedral is more fully explored.

8. See my *Sacred Places* (Simon & Schuster, 1991), and the chapter dedicated to the Jukuita cave.

9. Utta Malnic, with David Mowaljarlai, *The Spirit of the Kimberley*, unpublished manuscript.

10. W. Arndt, *The Dreaming of Kunukban*, Oceania Vol. 35: 4, June 1965.

11. Titus Burkhardt, *Sacred Art East and West*, Perennial Books, 1967. A copy of the *Mandilion* is preserved in Laon Cathedral.

12. Father Basil Krivosheine, '*The Ascetic and Theological Teaching of Gregory Palamas*', The Eastern Churches Quarterly, 1938, No. 4. 'God is not light according to substance, but according to energy.'

13. See Allamah Sayyid Muhammed Husayn Tabatab'i, *Shi'ite Islam*, Allen & Unwin, 1975, pp. 130–31 for an explanation on Qualities. 'By Quality of Action is meant that after the act of actualization of an act, the meaning of a quality is understood from that act, not from the Essence (that performs the act), such as "Creator", which is conceived after the act of creation has taken place.' We are seeing here a contrast between the willing of the world into existence by the All-father *Ungud* or *Mangela*, and its actual creation by the Rainbow Snake and other Sky Heroes. The Qualities of Action of the Rainbow Snake is its creation of the land. The Qualities of Essence are Ungud's willing, which reflects his essence. At the human level, a man's totem reflects his Qualities of Action, which in themselves derive their origin from Ungud's Qualities of Essence.

CHAPTER 5

1. Maurice Bowra, *Primitive Song*, Weidenfeld & Nicolson, 1962.
2. Compare with Ludwig Wittgenstein in *Tractatus Logico-Philosophicus*, Routledge, 1974, 'Thus people today stop at the laws of nature, treating them as something inviolable, just as God and Fate were treated in past ages. And in fact both are right and wrong; though the view of the ancients is clearer in so far as they have a clear and acknowledged terminus, while the modern system tries to make it look as if *everything* were explained.' (6.372)
3. Eric Vaszolyi, *Aboriginal Australians Speak*, Mt Lawley College of Advanced Education, 1976.
4. Quoted in the Introduction to *Flinders Ranges Dreaming*, Dorothy Tunbridge, Aboriginal Studies Press, 1988.
5. Ibid., p. 192.
6. Wittgenstein, op. cit., 6.522.
7. Tunbridge, Dorothy, *Flinders Ranges Dreaming*, Aboriginal Studies Press, 1988.
8. Ibid., p. 3.
9. Compare with Muhammed, in the *Bihar al-anwar*, Vol. III, from the *L'tiquadat* of Saduq, 'You have been created for subsistence, not annihilation. What happens is that you will be transferred from one house to another.' This bears comparison with the exit from the cocoon of the butterfly. Quoted in *Shi'ite Islam*, Allen & Unwin, 1975, p. 164.
10. Dorothy Tunbridge, op. cit., p. 6.
11. Ibid., p. 10.
12. James Cowan, *Sacred Places*, Simon & Schuster, Sydney, 1991.
13. For a detailed description of the *wunnan* system, consult *The Spirit of the Kimberley*, by Utta Malnic and David Mowarljarlai. Compare also Plato (Timaeus 30b): 'Let us admit that this world is a living being who has a soul, that it is a spiritual being and that in verity it has been engendered such by the Providence of God.'
14. Utta Malnic and David Mowarljarlai, *The Spirit of the Kimberley*, pp. 184–6.
15. Gustav Fechner, *Uber die seelenfrage*, etc, Hamburg and Leipzig, 1907. Quoted in Henry Corbin's *Spiritual Body and Celestial Earth*, Bollingen 41:2, 1977.

CHAPTER 6

1. R.M. Berndt, *Wuradjeri Magic and 'Clever-Men'*, Oceania Vol. 17, 1946–7.
2. B. Spencer and F. Gillen, *Native Tribes of Central Australia*, Macmillan & Co., 1938.
3. R.M. and C.H. Berndt, *The World of the First Australians*, Ure Smith, 1977.
4. R.H. Mathews, *Folklore of the Australian Aborigines*, Pamphlet, Sydney, 1899.
5. Also Abu Bakr Muhammed bin Tufail's work, *The Journey of a Soul*, Octagon Press, 1982. He speaks of the hero, Hai bin Yaqzan donning feathers from an eagle: 'The tail he placed on his back and the wings on his upper arms' so that the animals saw him as someone different. An angelic disposition is clearly intimated by the appearance of feathers. In the case of the *Karadji* he too is bestowed with the gift that enables him to 'fly away from his people' – in other words to remain apart, a figure of awe.
6. A.P. Elkin, *Aboriginal Men of High Degree*, University of Queensland Press, 1977.
7. Ibid., pp. 9–10.
8. A.W. Howitt, *Australian Ceremonies of Initiation*, Journal of the Anthropological Institute of Great Britain and Ireland, Vol. 13, p. 445, (footnote 1)
9. H. Basedow, *The Australian Aboriginal*, F.W. Breece & Sons, Adelaide, 1925.
10. B. Spencer and F. Gillen, *Native Tribes of Central Australia*, op. cit., p. 525.
11. Ibid. p 45. Flinders Ranges Dreaming.
12. A.P. Elkin, *Aboriginal Men of High Degree*, op. cit., p. 63.
13. R.M. Berndt, op. cit., p. 341.
14. Mircea Eliade, *The Two and the One*, Harvill Press, London, 1965.
15. A.P. Elkin, op. cit., p. 33.

CHAPTER 7

1. Ronald Berndt, *Three Faces of Love*, Nelson, 1976.
2. Ronald and Catherine Berndt, *Sexual Behavior in Western Arnhem Land*, Viking Fund Publications in Anthropology, No. 16, 1963.
3. Ibid., pp. 26–7.

4. B. Spencer and F. Gillen, *Native Tribes of Central Australia*, Macmillan & Co., 1938.
5. Ronald and Catherine Berndt, op. cit., p. 58–9.
6. Ronald Berndt, *Kunapipi*, Cheshire, Melbourne, 1951.
7. Roland Robinson, *Aboriginal Myths and Legends*, Sun Books, 1977.
8. See Ronald Berndt's *Three Faces of Love*.
9. All quotes are taken from Berndt's *Three Faces of Love*.

## CHAPTER 8

1. Howard Morphy, *Journey to the Crocodile's West*, Australian Institute of Aboriginal Studies, Canberra, 1984.
2. R. Schwaller de Lubicz, *Sacred Science*, Inner Traditions, New York, 1982, See pp. 216–22 where the author suggests that the 'Ka is the energetic fixity which is the magnet for the Ba.' Ka is the forces of life, the nutriments; Ba that spiritual dimension that must free itself from terrestrial (Ka) attachments demanding reincarnation. Ba here corresponds to the birrimbirr spirit.
3. Howard Morphy, op. cit.
4. W.L. Warner, *A Black Civilisation*, Harper & Row, Chicago, 1958.
5. J.C. Reid, *A Time to Live, A Time to Grieve*, Medical Journal of Australia ss 1:5, 1979.
6. This concept of an image 'not made by human hands' (Greek: *acheiropoietos*) finds its expression in other spiritual disciplines as mentioned in an earlier chapter.
7. Howard Morphy, op. cit.
8. I am reminded of a conversation I had with an Athonite monk where he informed me that prayers and singing performed at the foot of a dying man's bed are designed to ensure that the 'dark angel' be suppressed, and that the 'white angel' triumph at the moment of death.
9. Howard Morphy, op. cit.
10. R.M. and C.H. Berndt, *The World of the First Australians*, Ure Smith, Sydney, 1964.
11. B. Spencer and F. Gillen, *The Native Tribes of Central Australia*, Macmillan & Co., 1938.
12. See Margaret Clunies Ross and L.R. Hiatt's article 'Sand sculpture at a Gidjingali burial rite' in *Form in Indigenous*

*Art*, edited by Peter J. Ecko, Australian Institute of Aboriginal Studies, Canberra, 1977.
13. See Ian Keen's article, 'Yolngu sand sculptures in context' in *Form in Indigenous Art*.
14. B. Spencer and F. Gillen, *Across Australia*, Vol. 2, Macmillan & Co., 1912.

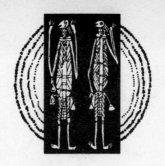

# SELECT
# BIBLIOGRAPHY

Primary sources have been listed in the Notes for each chapter. The following references, however, contributed to the background research of this work.

Bates, Daisy, *The Passing of the Aborigines*, Heinemann, 1966.

Beckett, Jeremy, *Torres Strait Islanders*, Cambridge University Press, 1987.

Berndt, Ronald M., *Kunapipi*, Cheshire, 1951.

Blake, Barry, J., *Case Markings in Australian Languages*, AIAS, 1979.

Broome, Richard, *Aboriginal Australia*, Allen & Unwin, 1982.

Capell, A., *Cave Painting Myths: Northern Kimberley*, Oceania 18, 1972.

Dawson, James, *Australian Aborigines*, George Robertson, 1881.

Dortch, C., *Devil's Lair*, A Study in Prehistory, Western Australian Museum, 1984.

Elkin, A.P., *The Australian Aborigines*, Angus & Robertson, 1974.

Hardy, Bobbie, *Lament for the Barkindji*, Rigby, 1976.

Kearney, G.E. & McElwain, D.W., *Aboriginal Cognition*, AIAS, 1976.

Kirk, R.C., *The Human Biology of Cape York*, AIAS, 1973.

Langloh Parker, K., *Aboriginal Legendary Tales*, Bodley Head, 1978.

Lawrie, Margaret, *Myths and Legends of the Torres Strait*, University of Queensland Press, 1970.

McKellar, Hazel, *Matya-Mundu*, Cunnamulla Australian Welfare Association, 1984.

Malnic, Utta and Godden, E., *Rock Paintings of Aboriginal Australia*, Reed Books, 1988.

Moore, David R., *Islanders and Aborigines of Cape York*, AIAS, 1979.

Mountford, C.P., *Brown Men Red Sand*, Angus & Robertson, 1948.

Mountford, C.P., *Nomads of the Australian Desert*, Rigby, 1974.

Moyle, R.W., *Songs of the Pintupi*, AIAS, 1939.

Reed, A.W., *Aboriginal Myths, Legends and Fables*, Reed Books, 1982.

Reed, Peter, *The Stolen Generations*, N.S.W. Ministry of Aboriginal Affairs.

Reynolds, Henry, *Dispossession*, Allen & Unwin, 1989.

Robertson, Roland, *The Man who Sold his Dreaming*, Rigby, 1977.

Turner, David H., *Tradition and Transformation*, AIAS, 1974.

Western Australian Museum, No. 2, *Depuch Island*.

Wright, RUS *Stone Age Tools as Cultural Markers*, AIAS, 1977.

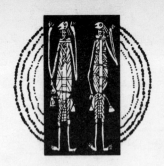

# INDEX